When Pigs Fly

I0103983

© 2020 by Stanley J. St. Clair
St. Clair Publications

All rights reserved. No part of this publication may be reproduced or transmitted in any form by any means electronic or mechanical, including telecopy, recording, or any information storage and retrieval system now known or invented, without permission in writing from the publisher, except by a reviewer who wishes to quote brief passages in connection with a review written for inclusion in a magazine, newspaper or broadcast.

ISBN **978-1-947514-24-9**

Printed in the United States o America by
St. Clair Publications
P. O. Box 726
Mc Minnville, TN 37111-0726

http://stclairpublications.com

Cover design by Kent Grey-Hesselbein,
KGB Design Studio
Manchester, TN, USA

http://kghdesign.nvaazion.com/

Interior images:

https://publicdomainvectors.org/en/

Picture title page: Stanley J. St. Clair

Picture page 7: Trula St. Clair

When Pigs Fly

The Humorous History of Animal Metaphors

Stanley J. St. Clair

Acclaimed author of the popular book series

Most Comprehensive Origins of Clichés, Proverbs and Figurative Expressions
and the newspaper column
Where Did that Come From?*

Edited by Michele Doucette

(*aka *Where Did that Saying Come from? Where Did it Come from?* and *Word Play* in various publications, in print and online)

Author's Introduction

For the past ten years I have studied and researched the origins of old sayings, metaphors, similes, clichés and other popular expressions which most English speaking people use without thinking about how they originated. Engaged in this fascinating study, I have been amazed at how many of them attributed folk etymology beliefs to their genesis, which have proven to be incorrect. Many others have been given an earliest attestation time by competent etymologists, which have also been wrong. I am far from perfect, so some of my research may also be a tad off, but I do try to be cautious when stating that my conclusions appear to be correct or likely. I do not see myself as the final authority on this subject. However, I do believe my books and articles to be among the most accurate, to date, in this field. My series of tomes appear to have transcended previous works as a printed body of research on the origins of English phrases, combined with those adopted into our popular jargon from other languages.

With familiar expressions inspired by members of the broad animal kingdom, this book of fun has been grouped in sections featuring phrases related to various classifications. I trust that it, too, will continue to inform and entertain my readers. As in the original works, please note that original period spellings and author misspellings have been retained. Some of these entries may surprise the readers.

Stanley J. St. Clair

Table of Contents

Section One: Around the House and Farm   **7**

    Dogs   **8**

    Cats   **28**

    Less Common Pets   **42**

    Pigs & Hogs   **43**

    Horses & the Like   **53**

    Cattle, Oxen, etc.   **78**

    Sheep & Goats   **89**

    Farm Fowl & Domesticated Birds   **94**

Section Two: The Jungle, Forest and Desert   **119**

    Savage Cats   **120**

    Wild Canines   **124**

    Primates   **127**

    Elephants   **133**

    Bears   **135**

    Dromedaries   **137**

Deer	138
Marsupials	139
Small Mammals	141
Reptiles	149
Section Three: Creepy Crawly Critters	**157**
Insects, Bugs & Such	158
Pesky Rodents	168
Section Four: Birds of a Feather	**171**
Beloved Birds	172
Dreaded Birds	178
Section Five: Fish & Other Water Creatures	**183**
Strictly Fishes	184
Other Sea Creatures	192
Alphabetical Index	**193**

Section One

Around the House and Farm

Expressions relating to man's furry and fine feathered friends

Dogs

It is often said that **a dog is man's best friend**. This seems to derive from the well-accepted fact that dogs are intrinsically faithful to their owners; we now know that those with pets are likely to live longer, according to those who do such studies.

The first known publication of this saying is from a poem published in *The New York Literary Journal*, Volume 4, 1821.

> "The faithful **dog**—why should I strive
> To speak his merits, while they live
> In every breast, and **man's best friend**
> Does often at his heels attend."

To paraphrase a quote from former British Prime Minister, Harold Macmillan, "Fido, 'you've never had it so good.'"

When we think of puppies, many of us have warm and fuzzy feelings. **Puppy love** is an informal term for feelings of infatuation experienced by adolescent males or females when coming of age, which may be either romantic or plutonic, but not usually one that develops into a lasting relationship. The term is often used jokingly, or in a pejorative sense, by parents or relatives of young boys or girls when expressing their first feelings for another person. It is so called because it is likened to the love a person could develop for a puppy.

Various songs have been written about this phenomenon, the earliest of which was the first single released by award-winning country artist, Dolly Parton, at age 13, in 1959. But the expression had been around since the dawn of the 20th century. A poem titled *Puppy Love*, about a real puppy, was published in a college yearbook in 1900; then, in 1908, William Marion Goldsmith used it figuratively in *Stones in a Life* in the title and first paragraph on page 115, and in several other places in chapter 8, 'Emily; or Puppy Love,' where it is seemingly presented as a recent term. The chapter begins:

"There comes a time in the lives of all boys and girls, too, when they have what they believe to be affections of the heart, but which older heads have termed '**Puppy love.**'"

No one knows who actually came up with the metaphor, but other early 20th century citations also use quotes, making recent coining very likely.

There are many sayings that we can derive from our canine friends. Treating them right should be everyone's pleasure. Unfortunately, not all people do that. But most of us probably don't wake one that is sleeping unless it is necessary. **Let sleeping dogs lie** is a metaphoric expression which means once a scenario has played out it is usually better to 'let well enough alone' than to try to change it and possibly instigate trouble and make matters worse for all concerned. It is a quote and favorite saying from first British Prime Minister, Sir Robert Walpole (1676 –1745).

But Sir Robert is not the originator of the saying. A form of it was used earlier by Geoffrey Chaucer in *Troilus and Criseyde*, published in 1374.

"It is nought good a **sleepyng hound** to wake."

Then, John Heywood, in his second book of phrases, *A Dialogue Conteynyng Prouerbes and Epigrammes*, in 1592, recorded it much the same as:

9

"It is ill wakyng of a **sleapyng dogge**."

The thought actually has its roots in the biblical book of *Proverbs, 26:17* (KJV):

"He that passes by, and meddles with strife belonging not to him, is like one that takes a dog by the ears."

One metaphor with which we are all familiar is **Dog-eat-dog**. Its roots are very old.

The *Gentleman's Magazine and Historical Chronical*, Volume XIX, 1749, on page 448 references a poet who said, 'nor will dog eat dog.' The Second Edition *Oxford English Dictionary* refers to a quote from 1858 of an old proverb, 'Dog does not eat dog.' Then in 1776, the following appears in *The Fall of the British Tyranny, or, American Liberty Triumphant* by John Leacock, on page 48:

"Kidnapper. Aye, so I've heard, but I look upon this to be a grand manœuvre in politics; this is making **dog eat dog**— thief catch thief— the servant against his master— rebel against rebel— what think you of that, parson?"

From this idea the current meaning likely evolved which was already understood by Saturday, December 25, 1813, when this appeared in *The Examiner* published in New York:

"All the trade and commerce we are to have is among one another: if any body makes money, he must make it, not by his enterprise in foreign commerce, but out of his own countrymen. '**Dog eat dog**,' is now our commercial motto and practice…"

This metaphoric phrase definitely refers to fierce competition; this is often obvious among dogs fighting over bones or food.

From the fact that some canines get defensive, and even have been known to bite their owners when going after food, especially when others are vying for it, comes the saying, **don't bite the hand that feeds you**.

This is another old one from at least the 18th century in England, for political writer, Edmond Burke, used a version of it.

> "...having looked to government for bread, on the very first scarcity they will turn and **bite the hand that fed them**."

However, this saying is likely much older, and means exactly what it sounds like. If someone is being kind to you, return the kindness, don't fight them.

It's certain, though, that when our canine friends get hold of a juicy bone, they are very possessive of it. Sort of like they are marking their territory or protecting their keepers. They hold onto it until every edible morsel is devoured. **Like a dog with a bone** is a vivid expression which refers to an unwillingness to stop thinking, talking about or dealing with a matter until it is resolved. Similes of persons acting like a dog with a bone go back to at least 1800, when Joel Chandler Harris used this comparison in his biographical sketch of the famed ambitious Atlanta newspaper magnate, *Life of Henry W. Grady*, page 258:

> "He hid about in the day-time, avoiding everybody, and seeming to carry off his love and his passion, as a **dog with a bone**, seeking an alley. At night he would be seen hanging **like** a guilty thief about the hut in which his treasure was hid."

Luckily, when it comes to being fierce with people, a lot of our furry friends are **all bark and no bite**.

Often said of someone who makes cutting remarks, this means full of big talk but lacking action, power, or substance. It was inspired by the fact that many dogs which bark a lot are actually afraid of people. This is a form of the saying '**His bark is worse than his bite**' from Anglican priest, George Herbert in his 1651 book of

11

proverbs. This saying, per se, however, began popping up in the mid-19th century. The earliest available reference is from *The African Repository and Colonial Journal*, Volume 23, page 41, February, 1847:

> "When the zeal of theories rises to the height of non-resistance, the danger to the nation is small. It is **all bark and no bite**. But a political parly implies the shedding of blood if deemed necessary; and when men set out with theories which cannot always be reduced to practice, as they could wish, they may find in the end that their theories will have a practice which they did not anticipate."

The gruff barking of dogs begat the saying '**barking orders**,' implying that someone is harshly demanding that others do their bidding. The earliest known example in print of this metaphor dates to 1907.

A more popular one, however, is **barking up the wrong tree**. This one is older, going back to at least 1832, when it appeared in James Kirke Paulding's *Westward Ho!*

> "Here he made a note in his book, and I begun to smoke him for one of those fellows that drive a sort of a trade of making books about old Kentuck and the western country: so I thought I'd set him **barking up the wrong tree** a little, and I told him some stories that were enough to set the Mississippi a-fire; but he put them all down in his book."

The English is a bit less than perfect in this reference, but the phrase must have caught on in the United States quickly after Hall's book. It appeared in several American newspapers throughout the 1830s. One notable example is in this piece from the Gettysburg newspaper *The Adams Sentinel* in March of 1834:

"Gineral you are **barkin' up the wrong tree** this time, for I jest see that rackoon jump to the next tree, and afore this he is a mile off in the woods."

And speaking of barking, there's another old proverb, **don't keep a dog and bark yourself**. This means that there is no need to pay someone to do a job you can do yourself. The earliest known citation is in the novel *Philotimus*: *The Warre Betwixt Nature and Fortune* by Brian Melbancke, 1583:

> "**It is small reason you should kepe a dog, and barke your selfe.**"

Another behavioral figure of speech refers to how fast a pet can run when it has been doused with hot water. **Like a scalded dog / cat**. Sometimes preceded by **run, take off** or **go**, and with various animals attached, this means to scurry with lightening speed. It goes back to the days when a lot of cooking was done outside, and animals came around looking for morsels of food. Sometimes boiling water would get knocked out of a cauldron and get on a household pet, causing an immediate yelp and dash for safer ground. It is used figuratively to mean someone is running away from unpleasant circumstances. The earliest known reference in print is like a scalded cat, and is from *Corbett's Two Penny Trash or Politics for thee Poor* by John Corbett, 1831, page 257:

> "...I will bet Mr. Attwood just what he likes; that he does not find, between Temple-bar and Bishopsgate, one single shopkeeper who would not **run like a scalded cat** and hide himself under his counter, if he were in danger of being exposed to endure what Mr. Attwood deemed such an honour."

'Scalded dog' comes 23 years later in *Westminster Abby* by Emma Robinson, 1854, Volume I, page 282:

> "'Nay, nay, we will not **run** the palace **like scalded dogs**! — Master Roodspere, methinks you should have some sense of his

grace's condescending, if but — Who is there?' exclaimed Cromwel, breaking off as a tap at the oratory door…"

There are several dog terms referring to being hurt, humiliated or scared. One is "**Lick one's wounds**." This means to recover from hurt feelings after a defeat, rebuke or criticism. It is based in the ancient Greek and Roman belief that saliva has healing powers, and the fact that animals do indeed lick their wounds to heal them. In *The Works of Samuel Johnson, L.L.D.*, 1787 we find:

> "Politics, the most vulgar of all topics, were alone excluded, The British lion was then **licking his wounds**, and we drank to the peace of old England."

Coming from stock dogs following cattle or sheep closely and **nipping at their heels** to urge them to move on, this metaphor is applied to business, professional, sports, or even academic rivals gaining ground on competition, threatening to overtake them. It has been applied figuratively since the mid-to-late 20th century, with early examples in sports. A great reference is found in the Brigham Young University student paper, *Daily Universe*, 12-14-1971, in an article at the top of page 11, 'Division titles fall as NFL race tightens':

> "Dallas has at least clinched a division title play-off with the Washington Redskins still **nipping at their heels**."

Tail between one's legs is used when someone has been humiliated, had their feelings hurt and pride damaged because of a clash with another party. It is derived from a dog which sticks its tail between its legs after it is scolded or hit.

This dates back to 1649 when it was used in *The Workes of that Famous Chirurgion Ambrose Parey* by Ambroise Paré and Adriaan van den Spiegel translated by Thomas Johnson, printed in London by Richard Cotes:

"And knowing hee had given him his death's blow, took again his long cassack, and went away **with his tail between his legs** and hid himself, seeing that the little man came not again to himself, either for wine, vineger, or anie other thing that was presented unto him; I drew near him, and felt his pulse which did not beat at all…"

Another version of this, **tuck one's tail and run**, is used to accuse someone of cowardice. The earliest known figurative reference to **tucking** one's tail is found in *The Meerut Universal Magazine*, Volume 1, on page 32, in verse IX of an admittedly unauthorized publication of the historic ballad, *The Devil Dutchman*, Agra, India, 1835:

"'Ha! ha!' said he, 'I'll take a tour to see the county's riches;
So he packed up his traps in half an hour
And **tucked his tail** in his breeches;"

And speaking of a dog's tail, you may have heard, **The tail wagging the dog**. This refers to the smallest or least important part of something controlling the larger or more important parts. The earliest known citation in print is in *The Memphis Daily Appeal*, in Tennessee, in May, 1871:

"Calling to mind Lord Dundreary's conundrum, the Baltimore American thinks that for the Cincinnati Convention to control the Democratic party would be **the tail wagging the dog**."

Lord Dundreary is a character in the play, *Our American Cousin* which was playing at the Ford Theater in Washington, DC when President Lincoln was assassinated there. In the late 20th century the term was shortened to '**wag the dog**,' developing a specialized political nature, spawning a 1993 novel and a 1997 film.

Dogs have served man since their domestication thousands of years ago. From the literal canine which is used to guard property comes the metaphoric term **watchdog**, meaning a person or organization which serves a guardian against waste, loss or illegal practices. It came into general use at the dawn of the 20th century. The earliest available citation is from *The American Monthly Review of Reviews*, August, 1902, in an article titled, 'Spooner of Wisconsin, A Sketch of the Present Leader of the Senate':

> "As a lawyer and maker of laws, as a **watchdog** against the furtive slipping in of blunders, as a suggester of stronger and better methods, as a deviser of practical schemes which will meet existing conditions in the Senate and the country, he is without a peer in public life."

But no dog has the needed skills to do everything. One metaphor focuses on this fact: **That dog won't hunt**. This means that a belief, theory or practice is not valid or practical. The earliest citation is from 1933 in Thames Williamson's *Woods Colt*, a novel about the Ozarks:

> "That feller is jest naturally a fool for the lack of sense, a-tryin' to mix whiskey an' lyin'. He ort t' of knowed **that dog won't hunt!**"

One reason some dogs won't hunt is because they are **gun shy**. When hunting dogs have had been frightened by a gun fired near them and would run at any loud noise they hide when they hear loud noises. This, as an idiom, means wary or mistrusting. Though later references were about dogs, the first verifiable citation in print refers to a breed of birds, and is in *Ornithological Rambles in Sussex* by Arthur Edward Knox, page 227, 1849:

> "Godwits then appear in their plain grey garb, and are all equally wary and **gun-shy** from repeated persecution…"

The earliest known totally figurative reference in print is found in *Peck's Red-headed Boy* by George Wilber Peck, page 42, 1901:

> "He has always been back with the women, taking up a collection. He has cared for nothing but money, and you will

find if they catch him, that his baggage consists of specie that he has stolen. **He is gun shy**, that is what ails Aguinaldo."

There are a lot more metaphors inspired by man's best friend. One is the expression, **dog and pony show**, stemming from the small travelling circuses of the mid-to-late 1800s, in America, such as Professor Gentry's Famous Dog and Pony Show, started in 1866. Over time this came to be a pejorative colloquialism for a highly promoted and likely over staged performance or event intended to sway public opinion for political or commercial causes.

When dogs start throwing up, it's often difficult for them to quit. Possibly hungry dogs getting into garbage cans in the days of old started **sick as a dog** being used figuratively of people.

This analogy, believed to have originated in the early 1700s when it was common to call something unclean or unwell a dog, actually began much earlier. Germs and disease were often spread by animals throughout history. This phrase was cited in print as early as 1592, when *Four Letters and Certain Sonnets Especially Touching Robert Greene* by Gabrielle Harvey contained the following in a poem titled 'A Due Consideration of the Quipping Author' on page 2:

"Now **sick as a dog**, and ever brain-sick,
Where such a raving and desperate Dick?"

The Australian expression for sick as a dog is **crook as a dog.**

There are at least three more proverbs about dogs beginning with "If you." The first one is: **If you can't run with the big dogs, you'd better stay on the porch**. This one means that if a person is unable to do what others are already doing, then it is best not to try. This is a proverb which has only become popular in recent years. Origin is obscure, but the earliest known citation is in *And the Sun Stood Still* by Guy Parish, 2002, page 101:

"They run like a scared Chihuahua back to the porch yelling, 'Oh, God, oh, God, oh, God!' **If you can't run with the big dogs, you'd better stay on the porch**.

But the others go back much further. First we'll look at **If you can't bite, don't show your teeth**. Unsurprisingly, like so many other old proverbs, this one has been attributed to various cultures. They include Yiddish, Chinese, French, and Scottish! It means that one should never threaten any action that he or she is not prepared to take. The earliest known actual listing of the proverb in English is in *Ames' Almanack* by Nathaniel Ames Jr., printed in the Bridgewater, Massachusetts in 1767, number 388:

"**If you can't bite, never show your teeth**."

This annual publication, started by Nathaniel Sr. actually enjoyed a much larger circulation than *Poor Richard's Almanac* by Benjamin Franklin.

Then there's "**If you lie down with dogs you get up with fleas**," which applies both to our furry friends and their pests! This proverb goes back to Latin, *Chi va dormir con i cani, si leua con i pulici,* and the earliest English version is in the 16th century translated by James Sanford in *Garden of Pleasure* in 1573:

"He that **goeth to bedde wyth Dogges, aryseth with fleas**.

Then, in George Herbert's *Outlandish Proverbs* (no. 343), 1640:

"Hee that **lies with the dogs, riseth with fleas**."

It means that if you associate with someone questionable, that person's problems will affect you in the long run.

While I was growing up I also heard that some people **have as many notions as a dog has fleas**. It is a now antiquated Americanism for a person who is unsettled and not able to stick to one path of action. It may have been coined by Jeanette Covert Nolan in her biographical book, *O. Henry, the Story of William*

Sidney Porter, 1943, but was likely in use in rural America before this:

"...at age eight, and soon to be nine, **had as many notions as a dog has fleas**."

Dog days of summer has nothing to do with dogs. It refers to Sirius, known as the Dog Star, which, to the naked eye, appears to be the largest star other than the sun, is invisible between 24 July and 24 August because it rises and sets at the same time as the sun. The ancient Greeks believed that this is what caused the exceptionally hot muggy days of summer during this period and dubbed them 'Dog Days.'

Perhaps the oldest dog expression is **dog in the manger**, which is popular in the U.K. It means 'spiteful and mean spirited,' and is especially applied to people who prevent others from having something that they themselves have no use for. Like so many old sayings, it is often credited to acclaimed fable-teller, Aesop (c. 620-564 BC). However, since some of these fables date back further than his lifetime, much doubt has been cast on the authenticity of his authorship. Actually, we now realize that the first version of *Aesop's Fables* were assembled and printed in German by printer Heinrick Steinhowel in 1480, then printed in English by William Claxton shortly thereafter, in 1484. *Dog in the Manger* was one of these fables, which portrayed a dog laying in a manger, not, of course, because he wanted to eat the hay, but, like the proverbial hog laying in the trough, wanted to prevent other animals from feeding on the hay. The fable of the dog in the manger was used twice by the 2nd century AD Greek writer Lucian of Samosata; first, in *Remarks addressed to an illiterate book fancier* and secondly in his play, *Timon the Misanthrope*.

John Gower, however, had published a version of this fable in English before Claxton, in *Confesso Amantis*, c. 1390:

"Though it be not the hound's habit

> To eat chaff, yet will he warn off
> An ox that commeth to the barn
> Thereof to take up any food." (Book II, 1.84)

It was used by at least one other Greek storyteller in the 3rd century AD, Straton of Sardis. A likeness of the basic tale was also cited in the apocryphal Gnostic **Gospel of Thomas**, discovered in Nag Hammadi, Egypt in 1945, where Jesus is quoted as having said:

> "Woe to the Pharisees, for they are like a **dog** sleeping **in the manger** of oxen, for neither does he eat nor does he let the oxen eat."

All we can say for sure is that the story is around 2,000 years old.

A platitude which is almost as ancient is **every dog has its day**.

Desiderius Erasmus (a medieval Dutch scholar) stated that this saying came about as a result of the death of Greek playwright, Euripides, who in 405 BC was killed by a pack of dogs loosed upon him by an enemy. It means that even a person whom others view as incapable of such action will at some time get revenge upon his oppressor, no matter how powerful the person may be.

Greek biographer Plutarch recorded a version of this proverb for what appears to be the first time in **Moralia** circa 95 AD, as 'Even a dog gets his revenge.' Richard Taverner, however, included the first English rendering, **'A dogge hath a day,'** in 1569 in his **Proverbes or Adages by Desiderius Erasmus Gathered out of the Chiliades and Englished**. The modern form of the saying appeared in John Ray's **A Hand-book of English Proverbs** in 1670 as **'Every dog hath his day.'**

Some dogs are brought up like royalty, especially those owned by aristocrats. **Putting on the dog** is an old metaphor, like 'putting on the Ritz,' which came later, means making a display of wealth or importance, particularly in flashy expensive clothing. It dates back to American college slang in the mid-19th century. By the 1880s it was well known. In the *Semi-Weekly Interior Journal*, Stafford, Kentucky, September 1, 1882, the expression appears in quotes on page 4 in a short article titled 'Too Fresh':

"For a week or two a pair of youths named Lehman, whose father is in the wholesale liquor business in Louisville have been here, and in the language of the street, have been **'putting on the dog'** quite extensively."

Dog leg is a metaphor used for a sharp bend in a road, or a harsh angle in a golf fairway. A major dictionary places origin at 1885 to 1890. It was, however, used to describe a flight of stairs which ascends to a half landing before aiming at a right angle and continuing upward as early as 1846 in *The Green and Grey*, Loyola University, Maryland, on November 7, on page 7 in Career Moves:

"Close-string in **dog leg** stairs, a staircase without an open newel."

A bend in a road was described as a dog leg as early as July 1, 1870 in *The Air Journal*, London, in The Rectification of the Kensington Road.

Crooked as a dog's hind leg implies that a dog has more crooked legs than other animals. That is likely because the knee turns backward, therefore it is thought unnatural. This means that a person is unusually corrupt. Mark Twain often gets credit for this in his *Letters from Hawaii*, 1866. It is possible that he used it earlier in a speech but there is an earlier citation in *The Amateur's Magazine*, November, 1859 in The Mammoth Grub, Part II:

"'Well, I can only say if it was the best, it didn't speak much for his mode of training 'em, for it was as **crooked**, sir, as a **dog's hind leg**. It was as **crooked**, sir,' lowering his voice to a confidential whisper, 'as some of his ways in business, and they're tortuous enough, I can tell you.'"

Dog's body, or **dogsbody** began as a British nautical term. In the early 19th century, the Royal Navy used dried peas and eggs boiled in a bag, known as pease pudding or pease porridge, as one of their staple foods. Sailors called this 'dog's body.' In the early 20th century, junior officers who performed tasks that senior officers didn't want to do became known as 'dogsbodies.' Likely this was because the pease porridge was something they didn't want to eat. About 1930, the term became somewhat common in non-naval situations.

Another clearly British and Aussie term is **dog's breakfast**. It has meant 'a complete mess' since early in the 20th century. This could have been derived from a botched attempt at making a decent breakfast which turned out to be something only a canine would consider fit for consumption, but the earliest known form seems to indicate that it had to do with appearance. It can be applied to any situation or project which has turned into an utter disaster. This appeared in *The English Dialect Dictionary* in 1902:

> Phr. (1) all in a lump like **a dog's breakfast**, said of a heterogeneous heap of things"

Hair of the dog is a common old colloquialism which refers to alcohol consumed to lessen the effects of a hangover. In the late 19th century, it referred to a method used to treat a rabid dog bite by placing hair from the dog on the bite area, but also was used for drinking. *Brewer's Dictionary of Phrase and Fable* by Ebenezer Cobham Brewer, published in 1898, page 570, contains the following:

> "In Scotland it is a popular belief that a few hairs of the dog that bit you applied to the wound will prevent evil consequences. Applied to drinks, it means, if overnight you have indulged too freely, take a glass of the same wine within 24 hours to soothe the nerves. 'If this **dog** do you bite, soon as out of your bed, take a **hair** of the tail the next day.'"

Brewer goes on to quote a poem to this effect attributed to Aristophanes, who lived circa 446 – circa 386 BC. However, 'hair of the dog' was applied as a cure to drunkenness in an even earlier ancient text from the city of Ugarit, now in Northern Syria, dating to the late second millennium BC, in which the Canaanite god Ilu becomes hung-over at a feast. In the text, as a cure, goddesses place the 'hairs of a dog' on Ilu's head and serve him a beverage made of parts of an unknown plant mixed with olive oil. The text was translated and published by Dennis Pardee in *Ritual and Cult at Ugarit*, 2002. This is very likely the true origin of the saying, which may have been passed down through the generations, as the Scottish have a legend that the ancestors of the Celts were Nomadic and originally came from the Middle East. Interestingly enough, this expression also is known to exist in Hungarian. Translated literally, it applies to curing a dog bite with its fur.

Another citation of interest which ties the two practices together is found in *The Life and Adventures of Obadiah Benjamin Franklin Bloomfield...Written by Himself*, published in Philadelphia in 1818, page 138:

> "And what do you think they came for? Why truly to initiate their *dupe* in the art of mysteries of dram-drinking; or to speak more fashionably, to teach him how to cure his headache by a repetition of the *indiscretion* which had occasioned it. 'A **hair of the dog** is good for his bite' — is a phrase in high repute, and well understood, amongst topers."

Going to the dogs has figuratively been used for anything going to ruin; for example, something which shows moral decay, since at least the late 18th century. A play entitled *Germanicus, A Tragedy* by 'A Gentleman of the University of Oxford' was published in *The London Review of Literature* in 1775, and included this citation of the phrase:

> "Sirrah, they are prostitutes, and are civil to delude and destroy you; they are painted Jezabels, and they who hearken to 'em,

like Jezebel of old will **go to the dogs**; if you dare to look at 'em, you will be tainted, and if you speak to 'em you are undone."

Then there is the popular saying, **the guilty dog barks first** or, **the guilty dog barks loudest**, which means that people try to cover up their wrongs by feigning innocence. When a group of people are confronted about which one did something, the one who immediately tries to point a finger and blame someone else is often the one who is guilty. Strangely enough, these sayings did not begin to be popular until the mid-20th century. The earliest such proverbs involve dogs that bark loudest. The first available citation is from the preface to English poet Terrance M. Hughes' lengthy ode, *Iberia Won*, chronicling the Peninsula War, published in 1847, where it is linked to a German proverb:

"**The dog who barks loudest is least inclined to bite**."

In 1902, we find a slight move in the axiom. In Bolsaw Prus and Curtain Jeremiah's historical novel of Ancient Egypt, *The Pharaoh and the Priest*, we find:

"Oho," said the pharaoh, "then they threaten me thus from the first day of my rein. My mother, **a dog barks loudest when he is afraid**; so threats are of evil omen, but only for the priesthood."

Most men have found themselves **in the doghouse** at one time or another. In chapter sixteen of Sir J.M. Barrie's *Peter Pan*, 1911, Mr. Darling, the father of Wendy, ended up chained in the dog's kennel as an act of personal penance for allowing the children to be 'kidnapped.' This is the first incident in literature of someone being 'in the doghouse' as a punishment.

The actual phrase, however, first appears in *Criminalese*, James J. Finerty's glossary of criminal jargon, in 1926:

"**In dog house**, in disfavor."

The idiom is often used as the place a man ends up when he has sorely offended his wife or significant other.

Men who have been so punished likely feel sorry for dogs. **Wouldn't wish that on a dog** is one of a number of this type expressions which started with "His worst enemy wouldn't wish that for him," in the Italian opera, *The Marriage of Figaro*, by French polymath Pierre Augustin Caron de Beaumarchais (1732-1799), first performed in Italian in Vienna in 1786.

On a short leash means to maintain control over someone. It is taken from having a dog on a leash in order to restrain and train it to obey commands. Figurative use came in the third quarter of the 20th century. An early example is in *Life Magazine*, November 10, 1961, in a caption under a photo on page 95:

"The U.S.S.R. made concessions to Polish nationalism but holds Gomulka and country **on a short leash**."

It's a dog's life was coined and popularized in past centuries when dogs guarded the homes in small communities. Winters were especially rough and the dogs slept outside. Life for them was not good, and was often short. The phrase meant that life was very bad. It is still used to mean that the tasks which have become one's lot in life are unpleasant but necessary. The earliest citation in print available is found in *Blackwood's Magazine*, October, 1847, in an article titled 'Hounds and Houses at Rome:'

"A '**dog's life**' has become a synonym for suffering; nor does the associating him with another domestic animal (If a second proverbial expression may be trusted) appear to mend his condition…"

Another saying which began quite differently is "**You need that like a dog needs side pockets**." But it is not nearly as old. This and other similar facetious analogies began popping up in American slang in the early-1960s. They obviously meant, 'you have no need of _____ whatsoever.' An early example is from the final act of Sidney Kingsley's three-act play, *Night Life*, first presented at New York's Brooks Atkinson Theater October 23, 1962:

"IGGY. Come on. **You need him like a hole in the head**."

The saying **You can't teach an old dog new tricks** is supposed to imply that younger people learn more easily, and this is usually true. This saying has become personified because the similarities between animal and human behavior patterns. But a lot of retired people have learned new skills and crafts.

The idea behind this saying has been around since at least the mid-17th century. It was recorded by John Heywood, in his 1546 book. The earliest reference to the idea from which this sprang, however, is from John Fitzherbert in *The boke of husbandry* in 1536.

"...and he [a shepherd] muste teche his dogge to barke whan he wolde haue hym, to ronne whan he wold haue hym, and to leue ronning whan he wolde haue hym; or els he is not a cunninge shepeherd. The dogge must lerne it, whan he is a whelpe, or els it will not be: for it is harde to make **an olde dogge** to stoupe."

'Stoupe' here meant 'put its nose to the ground and find a scent.'

Writing about all of these canine axioms has made me **dog tired**! This is another way to say 'worn out.' It refers to physical exhaustion, and is said to come from a tale of Alfred the Great, who reportedly sent his sons, Athelbrod and Edwin, out daily with his extensive kennels of hunting dogs. Whichever son was able to capture more of the hounds won the right to be seated at his father's right hand that evening at the Royal dinner table. Both sons came in 'dog-tired,' but happy in their accomplishment. It is recorded in Bede's *Historia Ecclesiastica Gentis Anglorum* Ecclesiastical History of the English People, 8th century, that the tradition carried on for the next few generations.

Cats

The other most popular "fur baby" is a kitty cat, and there are also lots of expressions which are feline inspired.

A carry over from the dog metaphor section is another one involving both of our beloved household pets: **Raining cats and dogs**. There are a number of theories as to the origin of this phrase, but it's been in use for centuries. One belief is that thunder and lightning represent a dog and cat fight.

Some say that in London, during the time of the bubonic plague, bodies of infected cats and dogs would wash up in the gutters during especially hard rains. Perhaps.

According to historians, however, this phrase was around back in the Dark Ages. Superstitious sailors believed that cats had a lot to do with producing storms; the witches who were said to ride the storms were often pictured on black cats.

Dogs and wolves were symbols of winds, and the Norse storm god, Odin, was frequently shown with dogs and wolves hovered around him. In the saying, 'raining cats and dogs,' cats symbolize the rain and dogs symbolize the wind.

Cats are notorious for getting skittish. That is where our next two expressions come from. **As nervous as a cat on a hot tin roof** has become the epitome of jittery and paranoid. It was actually coined as a result playwright Tennessee Williams 1955 hit Broadway play, *A Cat on a Hot Tin Roof.*

Strangely enough, the other one, as **nervous as a long-tailed cat in a room full of rocking chairs** came into existence about the same time.

This is a simile for being extremely touchy and jumpy at the least little thing. A cat with a long tail would be watching carefully to make sure a rocker didn't come down on its tail. Cats often twitch their tails when they feel that something may be threatening them. The earliest sources attribute this to Tennessee Ernie Ford, as this one from *The Antique Automobile*, 1955:

"Tennessee Ernie Ford says that driving on the freeways makes him as **nervous as a long-tailed cat in a room full of** people sitting in **rocking-chairs.**"

A classic rhetorical question, **Does a cat have a tail?** seems to have started in the mid-20th century.

One expression that is ever-popular among cat lovers is **the cat's meow**, meaning 'the ultimate' which was first coined by American cartoonist Thomas A. "Tad" Dorgan (1877-1929).

A similar expression is **the cat's pajamas**. At any rate, it means a really good thing, and sometimes a really good *new* thing.

One unlikely theory is that this saying came from E.B. Katz, an English tailor of the late 18th and early 19th centuries, who made the finest silk pajamas for the nobility and wealthy. But there just aren't any printed references available before the early 1920s of the phrase.

The expression has definitely been around since at least that decade. Some people think that cartoonist Tad Dorgan, the originator of 'the cat's meow,' first came up with it, as well as several others that didn't stick around including "the flea's eyebrows" and "canary's tusks."

Popular Science, January, 1926 edition, contained the following line in an endorsement for Daven radios by an editor:

"Man! — of all the beautiful, round and full tones, this is **the cat's pajamas**."

Some other people say that this phrase was coined slightly earlier than the 1920s, and used by schoolgirls. Tad Dorgan didn't invent it; he just picked it up and made it popular. The 1926 movie, ***The Cat's Pajamas*** starring Betty Bronson, Sally Winton, Ricardo Cartez and Arlette Marchal didn't hurt either.

There's not really any logical explanation for how or why it started, unfortunately. It was part of a popular series of phrases coined in the 1920s about animals and their body parts, including the bee's knees, the snake's hips, the clam's garter, the eel's ankle, the elephant's instep, the tiger's stripes, the leopard's spots, the sardine's whiskers, and the pig's wings. A forerunner of 'When pigs fly' (see) was recorded back in 1616. All of these are a bit silly. Whoever first came up with the cat's *pajamas* (obviously not a body part) might have chosen the word 'pajamas' because they were new and viewed as cool in the 1920s; but basically, they were just sticking with the fads.

Cats have nine lives is a common old saying based on ancient fables. Nine is a mystical number in folklore and many religions. Cats were revered in Egypt. The ancient Egyptian priesthood in On, mentioned in Greek literature as Heliopolis, worshiped Atum-Ra, the sun god who was said to be the giver of life. Atum-Ra, who took the form of a cat when visiting the underworld, was claimed to embody nine lives in one creator. The following is from an Egyptian song from the 4th century BC:

"O sacred cat! Your mouth is the mouth of the god Atum, the lord of life who has saved you from all taint."

Remnants from cat-worship lingered in Europe until the Middle Ages. Though the cat was no longer thought of as a divinity, they were seen as magical and otherworldly. The resilience of cats and their remarkable ability to survive is still an inspiration to humanity, so the myth of nine lives lives on.

From their attitude, it seems that cats haven't forgotten that. It has been said recently that **Dogs have owners, cats have staffs**. But still, the human race doesn't view them in quite that exalted a status. **A cat may look at a king** is a very ancient proverb that means that even a person of low social status has rights. The actual origin is obscure, but it is first found in print in *The Proverbs and Epigrams of John Heywood*, published in 1562:

> "Can ye judge a man, (quoth I), by his looking? What, **a cat may look on a king**, ye know!

A very familiar feline trait has always been their snoopiness. **Curiosity killed the cat** is a long-popular proverb which means that being too inquisitive can get a person into deep trouble. Precursors of the phrase first appeared in plays in the latter 16th century. In 1598 British playwright, Ben Johnson, used the following in the comedy, *Every Man in His Humour*:

> "Helter skelter, hang sorrow, **care'll kill a cat**, up-tails and all, and Louse for the Hangman."

About the same time, Shakespeare wrote *Much Ado about Nothing*, containing this line:

> "What! Courage man! what through **care killed a cat**, thou hast mettle enough in thee to kill care."

The precise saying appeared in James Allan Meir's *A Handbook of Proverbs, English, Scottish, Irish, American, Shakespearean and Scriptural*, 1871, in alphabetical order on page 34.

Fraidy cat or **scaredy cat** are equivalent forms of a colloquial Americanism for someone who is easily and unduly frightened; a coward. It comes from the fact that when a cat hears an unrecognizable sound or voice, it becomes immediately alert. It likely evolved from the pronunciation of "afraid" as early as 1816 in Africa and the East Indies, and according to etymonline.com goes back to 1871. The earliest available citation, however, comes from a poem on page 17 in *A Boy's Book of Rhyme* by Clinton Scollard, 1896:

"**FRAIDIE-CAT**

"I Shan't-tell you what's his name!
When we want to play a game,
Always thinks that he'll be hurt,
Soil his jacket in the dirt,
Tear his trousers, spoil his hat—
Fraidie-cat! Fraidie-cat!"

This poem later appeared in numerous poetry books, and was highly publicized, and was certainly the vehicle which popularized the term, if not the actual origin.

A later expression with the same meaning is **scaredy-cat**. In spite of conflicting sources, including a popular online dictionary which states origin at 1930-1935 and *Merriam Webster* which cites 1948 as earliest known usage, this term was in print as early as 1906 in the book, *Billy Bounce* by American author, William Wallace Denslow:

"'That is **Scaredy Cat**, and she will never come back.'"

When moving their young ones about, cats (and dogs) have a distinctive way of doing that. They bite down on the skin behind their heads and pick them up gently. I've never seen a kitten complain. **Take by the scruff of the neck** has come to be used figuratively to mean to take complete control of something or someone. The earliest literal citation available actually references a dog. It is from Thomas Hood's *The Comic Annual*, 1834, in 'The Rope Dancer,' page 2:

"However in they went, with a crash and a dash, and a grip and a grapple, and if they did not **take him by the scruff of the neck**, like a dog, there is no truth in St. Winifred's Well."

Figurative use came by the early 20th century. The first known example is from *Addresses Before the Eleventh Annual Convention of the Navy League of the United States* by Robert Means, 1916, page 43:

"...these two nations is reported to have once said, while we were engaged in war with Spain, 'If I had a larger fleet, I would have taken Uncle Sam **by the scruff of the neck.**'"

It has also been repeatedly used for taking charge of oneself; the earliest such example being only two years later in *The Outlook*, April 17, 1818, in 'After a Year at War,' page 8:

"The Happy Eremite, philosophizing amid the jubilant blades, recalled with an effort that he had work to do, took himself **by the scruff of the neck** and proceeded to his study."

When the mama cat is so loving to her young, they softly purr.

Purr like a kitten, as a metaphor, can have either of two meanings based on context. Most often it is applied to an engine, and means that it is runs very smoothly and efficiently. It can also refer to a person or group, extremely satisfied, and figuratively purring or moaning with pleasure. It has been in use since at least the early 20th century, and was used figuratively in 'The Return of Bill Garver', an article by David H. Talmadge, on page 4 of the Kentucky newspaper, *The Hartford Republican*, January 16, 1903:

"He was simply soaked full of love or whatever It is, and be was **purring like a kitten**."

Pussyfooting around is a figure of speech derived from the ability of cats to walk softly without alerting other animals, and even humans, of their presence. It means metaphorically walking around the true aim of one's intentions or opinions without coming to the point. It has been in use since at least the late 19th to early 20th century. *The Atlanta Constitution* used the term in an article on March 20, 1903:

"Vice President Charles Warren Fairbanks is **pussy-footing it around** Washington."

Because they get around so stealthily, cats historically played havoc with their prey. **A game of cat and mouse** is an idiom which has evolved over the past three hundred years plus.

This common expression is defined as a contrived action which entails constant chases, near catches and escapes. The basis is taken from an Indian Sanskrit tale of a lion, a cat and a mouse attributed to Hitopadesha about 1675, not to be confused with a much earlier fable by Aesop, *The Lion and the Mouse*.

Its use, as we know it, dates to the mid-to-late 19th century. It was first a literal game played in schools based on cats chasing and playing with mice as described in 1868 in *Chronicles of St. Mary's* by 'S.D.N.'

"Presently a girl left the players, who had just started **a game of 'Cat and Mouse**,' and seating herself by Lydia, showed she wished to make her acquaintance."

By World War I, it had begun to be used figuratively as seen in this snippet from the *Typographical Journal* in September, 1917:

"In those days it was a **game of cat and mouse**. We were the mouse and the Germans were the cat. They played with us. We never had any doubt as to the final outcome of the war, but we knew that for the time we were outnumbered, outgunned and outmunitioned."

Until the last few decades, it was common for house cats to go out in search of prey, whether mice, chipmunks, birds, or other small, helpless creatures. They had a tendency to proudly drag their find into the house all covered with their saliva, and a bit tattered, and knock it around playfully.

When someone not seen for a while would visit, possibly appearing weatherworn, a humorous greeting became **Look what the cat dragged in**.

Though the exact origin is unclear, this common saying has been around since the early 20th century and is freely used in both the U.K. and the U.S. An early example is from *The Railroad Telegrapher*, Volume 30, Part 1, 1913:

"Minnesota Division Notes: "**Look what the cat dragged in**. Brother D. J. Mahoney has resigned and the duties of division correspondent has fallen on my head."

Cat got your tongue? means, 'What's wrong, can't you say something about this?'

It is believed that this saying has its origin in the Middle East where, thousands of years ago, the practice of an eye for an eye was common. It was also customary to punish thieves by cutting off their right hand, and liars by ripping out their tongue. These body parts were fed to the king's pet cats.

A well-known attribute of male cats is that they love to roam around looking for needy females. **Tom-catting around** refers to a man who is 'on the prowl,' searching for 'hook ups' with numerous women. The earliest known citation is from *Dialect Notes, Volume 5*. 1927, page 478:

"**tom catting**, v. To seek illicit sexual adventure."

The earliest example of 'tom-catting around' in print, followed by many more from the 1940s forward, is from 1938, here in quotes, in *Southern Folklore Quarterly*, Volume 2-3, page 109:

"Kelly Combs said he learned this song at camp meetings when he was young and '**tom-catting around**.'"

Another trait of our dear feline friends is appearing innocent. **Looks like the cat that ate the canary** means a person who appears smug, especially while hiding something mischievous or private. The earliest known reference in print to a version of it is from 1910 in as article titled 'Cotton Bulls Stand Shock of Deliveries' in the *New York Times*, April 30th, on page 2:

"He talked freely and carried the smile of the **cat that swallowed the canary**."

Another universally known ability of our furry feline friends is their natural ability to survive a fall by hitting the ground on all fours! **Land on one's feet** is a common cat-inspired figurative cliché which means to have a successful outcome after a period of difficulty, especially in finances. It has been in use since at least the very early 20th century. The earliest available figurative citation, though in a slightly different context, is from *Historical Encyclopedia of Illinois* by Newton Bateman, 1903, page 838:

"He quoted Shakespeare, and referred to Caesar, Wellington and William H. Seward, and finally **landed on his feet** in dear old Rockford..."

Metaphors using cats with other creatures are universally popular. **When the cat's away, the mice will play** will be dealt with in the section on mice and rats!

Set the cat among the pigeons means to do or say something that one knows will cause unrest, alarm or controversy between a lot of people. *Cat Among the Pigeons* is the title of a novel by Agatha Christie first published in the UK by the Collins Crime Club in 1959. During British colonization of India (1620-1869), a popular pastime was to put a wild cat among a flock of pigeons. Bets were made as to how many pigeons the feline would kill. This was the inspiration for the saying.

Let the cat out of the bag is a very old expression. There are two commonly accepted origins for this idiom. The first and most likely is that it came from the days when piglets were sold at markets in bags, and some would put cats in the bags instead. To let the cat out of the bag would expose the fraud. This is also where the saying 'buying a pig in a poke' (see) came from, and is referenced as early as 1530.

Another theory is that the cat referred to a cat o' nine tails which was used to flog unruly sailors in olden days. Though doubtful, this is remotely possible, as there are references to the cat o' nine tails for centuries before any use of letting the cat out of the bag. The nine tails are from the three ends of rope which were each tied off in three more knotted ends. The 'cat' refers to the scratches made by the horrible lashes it cut in the flesh of the victim's back.

The term **Cat head biscuits** has an interesting origin. Biscuits, a type of which, known as the soft biscuit, was common in Scotland, came to be a viable type of bread in the Southern U.S. before the Civil War. In 1875, Alexander Ashbourne invented and patented the first biscuit cutter. A cathead biscuit, however, is a name applied to a large buttermilk biscuit, usually between six and eight inches around, made almost exclusively in the South, served with either gravy or butter (or margarine) and jelly, preserves or jam. They are crisp on the outside and fluffy inside. The term is believed to have originated in the Carolinas, and comes from the fact that they are normally about the size of a cat's head. The earliest known reference in print to these being called 'cat-head biscuits' is found in *Speaking to Persuade*, by LeRoy Brown, 1960, on page 74:

> "I shore like them **cat-head biscuits** and I want to sop gravy with you."

There are three very short terms including the word cat which are also entirely figurative. But the stories of the first two are much longer. Forms of the metaphoric expression **cat nap** have been used for 200 years to describe a short period of sleep during the day. Cats sleep long periods at a time, so it may seem strange to call it by this name. Some researchers say that it started in Ancient Egypt when cats were sacred and Pharaohs began to emulate the way cats sleep. But there are no records to indicate this. When cats sleep, they are sound asleep one minute and awake the next; there is no drowsy period trying to wake up; hence, the cat nap. The first use was actually 'cat's nap.' The earliest known citation is from *The Pioneers, or the Sources of the Susquehanna; a Descriptive Tale* by James Fenimore Cooper, 1823, on page 156:

> "Why d'ye see, Squire, the parson was very solemn, and I just closed my eyes in order to think the better with myself, just the same as you'd put in the dead lights to make all snug, and when I opened them ag'in I found the congregation were getting under weigh for home, so I calculated the ten minutes would cover the lee-way after the glass was out. It was only some such matter as a **cat's nap**."

Cooper used it the same way 2 years later in *Lionel Lincoln*, on page 111, 1825:

> "Wine should never slumber on its lees until it has been well rolled in the trough of a sea for a few months; then, indeed, you may set it asleep and yourself by the side of it, if you like a **cat's nap**. As orthodox a direction for the ripening of wine ..."

It continued to be cited in books as cat's nap for the next ten years, then in 1835, Harper and Brothers in New York published Matilda Douglas' *Blackbeard: A Page from the Colonial History of Philadelphia* in which contained the following at the beginning of Chapter XIX, on page 225:

"Towards two of the morning, not long after the moon had gone down, Nero, who was sitting up for his master, was aroused from a **cat-nap**, into which he had insensibly fallen, by a subdued murmur of rough voices, and a heavy tramp of many men passing along Penn-street ..."

In the late 19th century, three dictionaries were published listing 'cat-nap'. The first was *Americanisms, Old and New*, 1889, by John Stephen Farmer.

"**Cat-nap**. — This is given by Lowell as a short doze"

(Presumably famed American writer-poet John Russell Lowell)

The metaphor **Catwalk** today refers to a long, narrow walkway which runs between sections of an auditorium used by models to demonstrate clothing and accessories during a fashion show. Etymologists tell us that this word dates back to 1885. But it began with a different meaning. The earliest verifiable citation in print comes from *The Strand Magazine*, March, 1901, in 'Who Lives Next Door? The Legend of a London Street,' by George Manville Fenn, where the use is a bit different, seeming to be applied to either a garden path or a balcony on an apartment building, as the character in the drawing was staring out an upstairs window looking down at a garden:

"'The mystery increases,' I said to myself, and I descended with the intention of going out into our own **catwalk**; but mystery begat mystery, for I could hear the maids about, and seeking a screen for my very unusual proceedings I went into my study and lit my pipe."

Another reference that year by British author Douglas Sladen in his novel, *My Son Richard, Or, the Great Company*, applies it to a balcony; while *Highways and Byways in London*, by Emily Cook, 1903, has this citation:

"Such a London garden—a **catwalk** rather than a thing of beauty — is perhaps only redeemed from utter dreariness by an occasional plane-tree."

Later early 20th century references indicate a narrow walkway in a variety of settings, often around bodies of water; such as at a dock, a bridge or on a ship. Later ones are built around canyons and corrals used for cattle chutes.

It is actually late in the 20th century before primary usage of the term shifted to walks for models. *Textiles Technology to GCSE* by Jane Down, 1999, has the following under a photo:

"**Models on the catwalk** at a national fashion show at the Design Centre in Islington, London."

It may seem difficult to imagine how the word **copycat** came into usage. It likely started as a reference to the fact that kittens mimic the actions of their mothers. It is an Americanism and first known to appear in print in 1896 in poet S. O. Jewett's highly acclaimed book, *Country of the Pointed Firs*. From this reference it is obviously much older.

"I ain't heard of a **copy-cat** this great many years... 'twas a favorite term of my grand-mother's."

Pick of the litter now applies to getting first choice at a most-sought-after item. This idiom was derived from having the first pick of a litter of puppies, kittens or even piglets in the mid-19th century. The earliest known literal citation, speaking of Greyhound puppies, is from *Manual of British Rural Sports* Fourth Edition by 'Stonehenge,' page 161, 1859:

"I should care little as to the **pick of the litter** at weaning time."

The earliest known figurative reference is found in *If I were King* by Justin Huntley McCarthy, 1901:

"" 'Tis you who lie now,' grunted Tabarie. 'There's no gold issue in the world that would make you as cunning as François. You would never have done as he did if the king had made you **pick of the litter**.'"

Less Common Pets

A less popular household pet is a **guinea pig**. Metaphorically, a guinea pig is someone who is used, often to their own chagrin, as a test model for an experiment, the outcome of which may be iffy at best. It is unclear how the furry little cavy obtained this name back in the 17th century, for it is not a pig, nor did it originate in Guinea.

The earliest usage of this term to describe a person had nothing to do with the subject of an experiment, but was a novice worker on a ship in *The Adventures of a Kidnapped Orphan*, published in London in 1747:

> "He sent his nephew, at the age of fourteen, on a voyage as a **Guinea-pig**."

In the form which we now know it, it was first utilized by George Bernard Shaw in *Quintessence of Ibsenism*, in 1913:

> "...to the schoolmasterly vanity and folly which sees in the child nothing more than the vivisector sees in a **guinea pig**: something to experiment on with a view to rearranging the world."

Another 'pet' which is not as familiar as cats and dogs is the common **goldfish**. This term is used incorrectly to refer to someone who has a short memory. Actually, goldfish have a much longer memory than previously thought according to scientists.

Pigs and Hogs

As a whole, metaphors about porkers are not too positive. A person who is either dirty or self-indulgent is often referred to as a **hog**. **Hogging** things, particularly the bed covers, has long been used for the practice of taking more than one's share.

One of the common attributes folks think of when swine are mentioned is that they put on a lot of weight. This is not uniquely a characteristic of hogs. Likely because those who traditionally raised them to slaughter fattened them up! **Fat as a pig** has long been a metaphor for someone who has the misfortune of gaining more weight than is considered desirable. The use of this term goes all the way back to as early as at least the mid-1700s. British physician John Douglas used it in his *Short Dissertation on the Gout* in 1741, on page 20:

> "...and the child began to thrive from the first time he was anointed and soon grew as **fat as a pig**..."

Almost 100 years later, it was used in the famed nursery rhyme, *The Life of Jack Sprat* by John G. Rusher, published in 1840:

> "When Jack Sprat was young,
> He was not so big;
> But now he is old,
> And **fat as a pig**."

As I noted, pigs are fattened for slaughter. Because of this, and the fact that they are sold by the pound at market, another metaphor evolved. **Weighing the pig doesn't make it any fatter** is almost exclusively used in the U.K.

The earliest known citation in print, 'Weighing a pig doesn't make it *grow* any faster,' actually sounds like it could be the coining. It was not in a British source, however, but an American publication, *The Swine World*, July 5, 1919, in a story about a young boy in Iowa who told his father he wanted to weigh his pig every day:

> "'Why,' the father replied, 'you can't do that for we haven't any scale. Anyway, **weighing a pig doesn't make it grow any faster.**'"

In the story, the boy was insistent and the father told him if he could find a way to weigh the pig every day he would give him all the food necessary to feed it. The boy found a creative way to get the pig weighed, and got the feed, making the boy feel good about his accomplishment.

Speaking of killing hogs, in order to do so in the old days, farmers waited until it was very cold to slaughter them, then called in the neighbors to help. After they were cut in sections, the meat hung in what was called smoke houses or meat houses and salted to cure. In the book, *The Song of Sarah: Poverty and Plenty, Grit and Grace, Wit and Wisdom* by Charlotte Pillow Little, 2011, the true story is set in Arkansas in the late 1930s. The following is from pages 73-74:

> "In many rural areas, meats were still being processed at home on a cold, cold day in late December or January when the temperature dipped down to freezing or below, on a day when it was '**cold enough to kill hogs**,' as one old saying still goes."

Because of the belief that swine traditionally gorge down far too much food, **pig-out** has come to be used as an idiom for someone who grossly overeats. It came into common usage in the mid-

1970s. The earliest available example is in *Princeton Alumni Weekly*, November 24, 1975 in 'Class Notes,' on page 35:

"They came from Cape Cod, from Portland, from Miami, from L.A. to the biggest Italian-Jewish **pig-out** since Marco Polo first tasted chopped liver."

One thing for sure, when a porker gets full, he seems to be very contented, and many times is seen wallowing in the mud. As a result, a person who is in a very happy or satisfied state in which he or she has no worries or concerns is said to be in **hog heaven**. A major dictionary places first usage at 1944. The term was in use, however, by 1863, when it was cited in the *Report of the Commissioner of Agriculture* in Washington, DC, page 204, where it is in quotes, likely indicating that it was recently coined:

"In the height of the hog season in Chicago, in the neighborhood of the yards, it would sometimes seem as though we had almost got into a '**hog heaven**,' for, turn which way you will, in the cars, in the yards, in the streets, all is hog, hog; and their cowardly, pointed heads all turned eastward, running, grunting, squealing, and all showing a disposition to travel anyway but the direction wanted."

The above citation was actually related to hogs, though the use of 'heaven' was figurative. A very clearly metaphoric example, as used today, comes by 1904 in Elizabeth Robins' (C.E. Raimond) novel. *The Magnetic North* page 42:

"'Oh, let him alone. He's got a flask in his bunk, swillin' and gruntin'; he's just in '**hog-heaven**.'"

'High living' a phrase which had been in English vocabulary for many centuries as the lifestyle of the wealthy, began to be referred to in the early 20th century as **living high on** or **off the hog**. It is thought to have been derived from the fact that the better cuts of pork come from higher on the hog, as mentioned in this excerpt from the *New York Times* in March, 1920:

"Southern laborers who are 'eating too **high up on the hog**' (pork chops and ham) and American housewives who 'eat too far back on the beef' (porterhouse and round steak) are to blame for the continued high cost of living, the American Institute of Meat Packers announced today."

Eight years earlier, in 1912 in *History of Roanoke County*, page 29, by George S. Jack and Edward Boyle Jacobs this variant appeared:

"With all the tenderloin, spareribs and backbones, we **lived 'high off the hog**.'"

Another characteristic these popular farm animals are known for is their stubbornness. Although the term **pig-headed** was first used as early as 1756 as 'resembling a pig,' and referred to the pig-headed armadillo. But within a few years it came to mean obstinate and stubborn to the point of stupidity. The first known citation to the current meaning was in Francis Grose's *A Classical Dictionary of the Vulgar Tongue*, Second Edition, 1788:

"**Pig-headed**. Obstinate."

When pigs are injured or slaughtered they are known to bleed profusely. **Bleeding like a stuck pig** is a cultural phrase to describe profuse bleeding caused by a hog slaughtering technique in which the swine is stabbed in a main artery, usually with an anticoagulant on the instrument used.

The metaphor was in use by 1857 when it appeared in a British short story book, *Bentley's Miscellany Volume XLI*, in a tale called "A Fisherman's Third Letter to His Chum in India":

"You hit him, sir," said Tim, "for he is **bleeding like a stuck pig**."

After the turn of the century a version was listed in 1902 in *Slang and its analogues past and present*:

"Bleeds like any stuck pig."

Novels soon included it, and then it was used in a 1921 issue of *Saturday Evening Post*.

Hogwash is a very old term meaning nonsense, and came from a combining of the words hog and wash as early as the mid-15th century, at that time referring to slop from the kitchen fed to pigs. By early in the 18th century, the word was extended to also mean cheap liquor. In *The New Universal English Dictionary*, 1760, by Nathan Bailey, Fifth Edition, we can see how this evolved:

"TAPLASH, wretched, sorry Drink, or **Hogwash**."

Then gradually it began to be used for inferior writing, leading to its current connotation. A good printed example comes from *The Free Review, A Monthly Magazine*, edited by John M. Robertson, March, 1894, in 'Francis Adams':

"Carlyle's dyspeptic scoff at the philosophy of **Hogwash** finds no countenance from Adams, who by no means accepted Carlyle's inverted logic in this matter, as the lines hereunder show ..."

Male chauvinist pig is a somewhat archaic derogatory term which was coined in the early 1960s and used extensively in the 1970s by feminist groups to describe a man who exhibits an attitude of male superiority and disdain for women, especially in an aggressive manner. The word chauvinist is derived from the French *chauvinism*, after Nicholas Chauvin, proclaimed to be a legendary French soldier in Napoleon's *'Grand Armée'* (1805-1815). The word was popularized in Cogniard's vaudeville in the early-to-mid 19th century.

The earliest verifiable citation of this expression is in Mel Brooks' musical play, *All American*, 1962:

"TRISH. Maybe he isn't a **male chauvinist pig**."

From time in memoriam, hogs have never been noted as the smartest of animals.

Don't cast your pearls before swine is from the Bible, and these are the words of Jesus to Peter in *Matthew 7:6*. He is making the point to not waste wisdom or truth on people who are not prepared to receive it.

Buying a pig in a poke refers to the time when piglets were sold at market in bags. Since a cat was about the size of a young pig, unscrupulous merchants would sometimes defraud the buyer by placing a cat in the bag. Eventually it was no longer prudent to **buy a 'pig in a poke.'**

Today it is used to refer to buying anything 'sight-unseen.'

Another strange hog expression became popular in the mid-20th century on farms in the Southern U.S. Something which had no apparent reason for being where it was, was said to be **as useless as tits on a boar hog**. According to a major phrase origin book, this simile has been in use since the 1940s. The earliest available citation in print is in North Carolina author and columnist, Robert Ruark's novel, ***The Old Man's Boy Grows Older***, 1957, page 21:

"Them rich playboys is **useless as tits on a boar**."

Later references also included bulls, horses, etc.

Though hogs are notoriously greedy, and have been known to lie down in a feeding trough to keep others from getting any feed, that's not where **whole hog or none** comes from. It means that something to be done should be done properly and not halfway. To go whole hog is derived from Southern pork barbeque, where the entire hog is cooked. One of the earliest figurative citations of the phrase is in 1849 in ***Report of the Debates and Proceedings of the***

Convention for the Revision of the Constitution of the State of Kentucky, page 376:

"Do, at least, let us be consistent. To use a homely phrase, 'I want to go the **whole hog, or none**.' Let the people have the whole power of electing whom they wish."

Hogs are also commonly known to attempt to dig out of their lots by rooting with their sturdy snouts under the fence or sty. For this reason most farmers have traditionally put rings in their noses. **Root hog or die** is a common American saying dating to prior to 1834. It means that one must look out for oneself, because no one else will do it for you. The earliest known citation is in David Crockett's autobiographical book, *A Narrative of the Life of David Crockett of the State of Tennessee*, pages 117-118, where he called it 'an old saying':

"We know'd that nothing more could happen to us if we went than if we staid, for it looked like it was to be starvation any way; we therefore determined to go on the old saying, **root, hog or die**."

Several anonymous popular songs with this theme were published before the Civil War, some patriotic, some minstrel, and several since. The earliest, published in Philadelphia in 1854, opens with this verse:

"I'll tell you a story that happened long ago,
When the English came to America, I s'pose you all know,
They couldn't whip the Yankees, I'll tell you the reason why,
Uncle Sam made 'em **Root Hog or Die**."

There are several proverbs about these greedy, stubborn, fat, free-bleeding, yet tasty porkers. Mostly about what you can, can't, should and shouldn't do.

Never try to teach a pig to sing; it irritates the pig and wastes your time is a quote from *The Notebooks of Lazarus Long*, by Robert Heinlein (1907-1988), which has become proverbial. It is used to refer to someone with an annoying habit which they are unable or unwilling to change.

Never wrestle with a pig. You both get dirty, but the pig likes it is a proverbial saying which has often been misattributed; this time to Abraham Lincoln. The earliest form of it in print is found in *Moving Ahead on Your Job:A Guide to Success in Your Work*, by Richard P. Calhoon, 1946, page 171:

> "And when you begin refuting one another's reasons, fussing back and forth, you generally do what a nationally known industrial relations authority warns you against: you wallow in the mud with the pig. He says, '**Never wallow in the mud with a pig, because the pig likes it**.' That is exactly what he wants, because you are on his home ground. He can think of arguments as well as you can, so where do you come out?"

In his 1949 book, *Problems in Personel Administration*, on page 449, Calhoon, attributed the saying to Cyrus S. Chang, Director of the U.S. Federal Mediation and Concilation Service under President Harry Truman.

Then there are the ever-evolving proverbs about the idea that a pig will always be a pig. **You can put lipstick on a pig but it is still a pig** is a variant of the '**can't change a pig**' cliché which was only coined in the late 20th century. It means that attempts to alter a faulty product are futile. The premier offering was 'None can make goodly silke of a gotes fleece.' It was coined by Alexander Barclay in *Certayne Eglogues* in 1515. This was quickly altered in 1579 by Stephen Gosson in *The Ephemerides of Phialo* who wrote of 'seekinge too make a silke purse of a Sowes eare' from which evolved the yet-popular **You can't make a silk purse from a sow's ear**. Then Thomas Fuller, a British physician, noted the phrase 'A hog in armour is still a hog' in 1732 in *Gnomologia*,

Adagies and Proverbs, but it was already in print in Captain John Stevens' *A New Dictionary of Spanish and English and English and Spanish* in 1726:

"**An hog in armour is still but an hog.**"

Francis Grose's *Classical Dictionary of the Vulgar Tongue* in 1796 stated that a 'hog in armour' alludes to 'an awkward or mean looking man or woman finely dressed.' Evangelist Charles Spurgeon, in his *The Salt-Sellers*, 1887, recorded a variation:

"**A hog in a silk waistcoat is still a hog.**"

I even coined a new one in my original volume of *Most Comprehensive Origins of Clichés, Proverbs and Figurative Expressions*: "**You can feed a pig white truffles, but that doesn't make him a connoisseur.**"

And along this vein, we have the popular old saying **Even a blind pig finds a nut once in a while**. Used with either hog or pig, the animal usually favored in older texts, and sometimes it is a truffle, a chestnut or an acorn. This saying infers that no matter how inept at what someone is doing, he or she will get lucky every once in a while and do something right. Its origin, however, is obscure, though Jon R. Stone in *The Rutledge Book of World Proverbs* (2006) calls it Russian. It is used a lot on websites, in business, and most particularly concerning sales people who don't adapt well to the business, and by those inclined to think gambling or playing the lottery just might pay off some day.

Versions of it have been around in English since before it appeared in print as a saying in *Golden Hours*, a magazine for boys and girls, in January, 1877:

"**If 'a blind pig finds an acorn now and then,' as the saying goes, do you think we may safely say a blind hen finds a corn occasionally?**"

51

And finally, the comical expression which inspired this book: **When pigs fly**. When this phrase is used, the speaker has no hope that the matter being discussed will ever reach fruition. This current version was not the first. The original saying was recorded in John Withals' Latin American dictionary, *A Short Dictionarie for Younge Begynners* in the section on proverbs, page 593, 1616 Edition only.

"**Pigs fly** in the ayre with their tayles forward."

This expressed sarcasm and the thought that some folks were exceedingly gullible.

Thomas Fuller, in *Gnomologia,* in 1732, got a bit closer to our present meaning.

"That is as likely as to see **an Hog fly**."

Then in 1835, in *The Autobiography of Jack Ketch*, by Charles Whitehead, we find:

"Yes, **pigs** may **fly**, but they're very unlikely birds."

Like so many others, it has evolved to what it is today.

𝓗𝓸𝓻𝓼𝓮𝓼 𝓪𝓷𝓭 𝓽𝓱𝓮 𝓛𝓲𝓴𝓮

Equidae is the taxonomic family of horses and related animals. But most people probably wouldn't know them by that name, so I will just call them 'horses and the like.' This family of servants to mankind is one group that, like dogs, has more metaphors than most. The Americanism **as healthy as a horse** comes from the image built around horses in the 19th century as a symbol of strength and physical capacity; the one which later caused 'horsepower' to be used as the unit of measuring the power of a gasoline engine. It was in use prior to this, but the earliest verifiable citation comes from the American Edition of the international magazine, *The Review of Reviews*, November, 1891, in an article titled William II, Emperor of Germany, by W.T. Snead:

> "The Kaiser avoids the disorders which told so disastrously upon the iron constitution of Peter, and with the exception of the abscess in the ear, he seems to be as **healthy as a horse**."

The common feed of horses which were well cared for has traditionally been oats which made them healthy and playful. **Feeling one's oats** came to be used for people when they feel robust. Horses were fed with beans and fodder back as far as ancient Rome, and when they were peppy, they were 'full of beans.' The expression **feeling your oats** only came into use about two hundred years ago. At first it was referring to horses. On May 22, 1898, *The Daily Kentuckian*, a Hopkinsville, Kentucky newspaper, in an article titled 'Lieut. Comes Home for New

Recruits' on page 2, there is an figurative example about soldiers sleeping in a barn, but not eating hay like the horses, but **"few of them"** were **"feeling their oats."**

General Mills used '**He's feeling his Cheerios**' (an oat cereal) in their ads from 1950 to 1953.

Speaking of horses being playful, **horsing around** is a metaphoric idiom derived from this trait. It is similar to the term **horseplay**, meaning mischievous antics. When horses are together in a pasture or a corral, they wag their heads, buck around and playfully nip at one another. When children are together, they do a lot of the same things on a more human level. They pretend to fight and cut up with one another, hence, **horseplay** and **horsing around** were coined to describe this activity. The term **horseplay** is said to have originated in the late 16th century. The *O.E.D.* states 1589. However, actual printed evidence of usage of **horsing around** per se does not appear until the early 20th century, as in this first available citation in the January, 1904 issue of *The Threshereman's Review*, St. Joseph, MO, in an editorial review on page 24:

> "The method of working live steam in the low pressure cylinder is a good thing when you get in a tight place. But **horsing around** over these rough Illinois roads we have here with so much steam pressure as required is dangerous and shortens the life of a boiler."

Even this seems a bit semi-figurative. Then in the January 6[th,] 1909 issue of New York's *Puck* magazine, there is mention of 'hobby-**horsing around** the room on the broomstick,' which may have led to the more metaphoric usage of merely 'horsing around' as we know it. In 1925, Corey Ford's witty tale, *Three Rousing Cheers for the Rollo Boys*, had the apparent first actual example of **quit horsing around**: George H. Doren Co.

"'Come on, **quit horsing around** now, Ben,' warned Dick in a voice that boded ill. Whack! went Tom's bat against the third ball…"

Another playful thing horses and their kin do is kick up their heels.

Kick up one's heels is an idiom in America which refers to having a vigorously entertaining time doing things one enjoys. It likely originated from horses, when released from a stall, kicking up their hoofs in seeming celebration. The earliest citation is from the allegorical work, *A Hue and Cry after Conscience or The Pilgrim's Progress* by Candlelight, 1681, written by Father John Dunton, on page 49:

"Now had they known the remedy, all that had gone beside my pocket, nay, sometimes I have (especially when I have the guilt come fiush) made 'em sick as well as I have found occasion, keepin' 'em on the Rack for my advantage, by perpetual Physics till nature weakned, and the powrs of life decayed, they en'e **kicked up their heels**, and bid good night to ye."

In British English, it may also refer to waiting impatiently to be summoned. This apparently is derived from foot tapping that people sometimes resort to when made to wait impatiently for something. The following first reference to this is from Samuel Foote's *The Minor*, 1760, page 56:

"I suppose, this is a spice of *your* foreign breeding, to let your uncle **kick up his heels** in your hall, whilst your presence chamber is crowded…"

This version is also used now as 'kick one's heels.'

Because horseback riding has been practiced since before Christ, several clichés have arisen about this practice.

Riding high often means feeling immensely euphoric, possibly exhibiting an egotistical attitude. It may also apply to such feelings experienced from the effects of drugs. Sometimes it is used to mean enjoying great success, which was the first figurative meaning. The earliest citations of **riding high** date as far back as the 18th century, many poetical, and refer to heavenly bodies, and later, birds, then ships riding high on waves; giving us a glimpse of how the metaphor developed. The earliest figurative reference comes on Saturday, February 28, 1846 in *Chambers' Edinburgh Journal* in the feature, 'Cromwell in Scotland':

> "It is touching to hear these moans from the spirit of a man who to the world appeared as **riding high** in a position of great glory."

Another one using the word 'high' is **Get off your high horse**. For hundreds of years, one definition of 'high' has been 'powerful,' and 'out of touch with the common people.' The 'High Kings' of old often held commoners in contempt. Ancient rulers and lords rode large expensive steeds when surveying their kingdoms. Great military men throughout history rode such animals as well. They were viewed as above the law, haughty and untouchable.

To say 'get down off your high horse' implies that the speaker feels that the person being addressed is acting in a haughty or self-righteous manner.

The earliest references to high horses, like many idioms, were literal. The original ones were huge, and in medieval England they were known as 'great horses.' In Old English, John Wycliffe wrote thusly of them in *English Works*, circa 1380:

> "Ye emperour... made hym & his cardenals ride in reed on **hye ors**."

'Hye ors,' of course, translates to '**high horse**.'

By the 18th century, the term, 'mounting one's high horse,' was used in a figurative sense. In 1782, Admiral Sir Thomas Pasley penned his *Private Sea Journals*, which contained the phrase in this light. They remained unpublished for about a century and a half. In 1931, they were finally published by his great-great-great-grandson.

"Whether Sir George will mount **his high Horse** or be over-civil to Admiral Pigot seems even to be a doubt with himself."

Rode hard and put up (or **away**) **wet** means someone has been treated badly or abused. It is derived from horses being ridden past the logical limit, then being put in the stall without even being brushed and allowed to cool down, thus being treated very poorly.

The oldest verifiable printed reference to the American form is in *Texas Magazine*, March, 1974 on page 44, in 'Rodeo Madness' by Gary Cartwright:

"In cowboy talk, he looked like he had been **rode hard and put up wet**."

The earliest available, however, of the version normally thought to be British, is also from an American publication, *Field and Stream*, May, 1989, in an article titled 'Thoughtless Packing' by Steve Netherby on page 76:

"It's been '**rode hard and put away wet**' over many years and has always come through."

Note that both versions utilize the incorrect verb tense.

Riding off into the sunset is a dated pop-culture cliché which is derived from the American Western literature and films most popular from the 1920s through the 1970s. In such stories, a hero or heroes came into a small western town in which there were outlaws whom the locals were sorely unequipped to handle. After the heroes captured or killed the villains, they would ride toward they west, disappearing into the sunset; thus the expression came to typify a job well done and the end of the story. Though the term was mostly viewed in movies, rather than printed, an example in print comes from the children's classic, *Seven Day Magic* by Edward Eager, 1962, page 172:

"And mounting the giant's horse he **rode off into the sunset**."

As a cliché, a hobby horse is something that one dwells on, a fixation. Someone **riding a hobby horse** is harping on something that a lot of other folks would rather not hear about.

A literal hobby horse is a child's toy and consists of a long slender stick, much like a broomstick, with an imitation horse's head for a top. In the U.K., more detailed and lifelike hobby horses vary in style, one of which has been around since at least the early 17th century. They are particularly associated with May Day celebrations, and what are known as Mummers Plays (seasonal folk plays) and the Morris dance (a form of English folk dance accompanied by music).

Riding shotgun is a riding metaphor which does not involve being on a horse's back. This term has been used figuratively since at least the mid-20th century to describe sitting in a moving automobile next to the window on the passenger's side. It is derived from the person sitting next to the driver on a stagecoach; then called the 'shotgun messenger,' who watched out for would-be robbers. In spite of the claim on the most used online encyclopedia, which quoted another source, saying that the phrase was 'not coined until 1919, then appeared in print later,' it was first printed in 1905 by Alfred Henry Lewis in *The Sunset Trail*, page 349:

"Wyatt and Morgan Earp were in the service of the Express Company. They went often as guards — **'riding shotgun**,' it was called — when the stage bore unusual treasure."

When traveling by horse-drawn carriages was the primary means of transportation, the driver had to maintain a tight grip on the reins which were attached to the bridles in order to control the horses.

Take the reins, somewhat like 'take the bull by the horns,' infers taking charge of a situation; this has to do with assuming control of an organization or a government. Here, the obvious derivation is the correct one. The earliest known citation of figurative use of this term is found in James Tyrrell's *The General History of England, both Ecclesiastical and Civil: Containing the Reign of Richard II*, 1703:

"...so that as his Government was much disturbed by popular Insurrections, and rendered unsuccessful, by the jarring Councils and ill Management of his Governors, during his Minority; so, when he came to **take the Reins** of the Government..."

When preparing a horse to either ride of pull a wagon, it is necessary to put a bridle on it. **Take the bit between one's teeth** is an ancient saying which, like **Take the reins** also means to seize control of the situation. A bit is the metal part of a horse's bridle placed in the mouth to control the horse's movements when the reins are pulled to one side. By biting down on the bit, a horse can gain control back from a person.

The earliest known citation of this figurative term is under expressions having to do with 'dents' (teeth) in *A Dictionary of the French and English Tongues Composed by Randle Cotgrave*, 1611:

"Prendre le frein aux dents. To **take the bit between** his **teeth**;"

The above shows that it was already in use in both French and English at that date. It was utilized in *The Metal* by John Dryden, 1682:

> "But this new Jehu spurs the hot-mounted horse, Instructs the beast to know his native force, To **take the bit between his teeth** and fly To the next headlong steep of anarchy."

Saddle with, as a metaphor, means giving someone a burdensome task or indebtedness; something difficult to deal with. Saddling a horse, or other 'beast of burden,' is putting something on its back. The word saddle came into Old English before 900 AD as *sadol,* and derived from Old Norse *sothul* and Old High German *satul.* Figurative usage use of *in the saddle* (in an active position of management) is attested from the 1650s. This particular phrase was in use by the first half of the 1800s. It was already known before it appeared twice in *Biography of Edmond Pendleton Gaines* by 'A Friend' published in 1844. The first citation was on page 6:

> "It is but truth to say, that had General Gaines stipulations with the Sac and Fox chiefs been attended to properly, the country never would have been **saddled with** the expenses of the Black Hawk War."

There are two very ancient sayings using a beggar in conjunction with horses. One of these is **If wishes were horses, beggars would ride**. This proverb means that if wishing could make things happen even the most destitute people could have anything they wanted. It is based on a line from an old nursery rhyme, the first version of which was published in 1605 in *Remaines of a Greater Worke, Concerning Britaine*:

> "If wishes were thrushes beggars would eat birds."

The earliest version with horses was printed in James Carmichael's *Proverbs in Scots* in 1628:

"And wishes were horses, pure (poor) men wald (would) ride."

After appearing only a bit differently in John Ray's *Collection of English Proverbs* in 1670, the modern version appeared in James Kelly's *A Complete Collection of Scottish Proverbs* in 1721.

A **beggar on horseback** is used to describe an upstart; a person who has suddenly risen in the world and displays no manners.

The earliest mention of this is a proverb first recorded by Robert Burton in *Anatomy of Melancholy*, 1621:

"Set a **beggar on horseback**, and he will ride a gallop."

In 1650, John Trapp included the following in *Solomonis Panaretos; Or a Commenitarie upon the Books of Proverbs, Ecclesiastes, and Song of Songs*:

"The Crown of the wise is their riches; but yet give them a foole, you put a sword into a mad man's hand; the folly of such fools will soon be upon foolishnesse. Why? Was it not foolishnesse before they were rich? Yes, but now it is become egregious foolishnesse. [*Greek* quotation omitted] the earth cannot beare insolencies of such. Set a **beggar on horseback**, &c."

Other versions are mentioned by Dwight Edwards Marvin in *Antiquity of Proverbs*, 1922, page 246:

"'Put a **beggar on horseback** and he does not ride he gallops,' – Dutch

'Set a **beggar on horseback** and he will ride to the devil.' – English"

Forms of the proverb have been used through the ages by such authors as Charles Dickens (*Our Mutual Friend*, 1865) and Peter Pindar (*Epistle to Lord Londsdale*, 1792).

The old proverb, **Don't change horses in the middle of the stream** means to not make a major change in the midst of a campaign or project. Throughout the years variations of this proverb have often been used to promote incumbents in American political campaigns.

Most often, Abraham Lincoln receives credit for coining this phrase. This is not true, though he did popularize it in the English language. On June 9th, 1864, he was making a speech in reply to a delegation from the National Union League who was informing him of his nomination for reelection to the presidency, and offering congratulations, when he spoke these words:

"I have not permitted myself, gentlemen, to conclude that either the Convention or the league have concluded to decide that I am the best man in the country; but I am reminded in this conclusion, of a story of an old Dutch farmer, who remarked to a companion once, **it was not best to swap horses while crossing streams**."

A slightly different version of the speech was reported the following day in a number of newspapers, including the *New York Tribune*, leaving out his reference to the 'old Dutch farmer,' and leaving the readers to assume that he had coined the phrase. And there have been many variations since as to the actual quote.

Irrefutably proving that Lincoln did not originate this proverb, the *Hamilton Intelligencer* in Butler County Ohio, contained the following on September 10, 1846, as part of a story also in a political context:

"**No Time to Swap Horses**. There is a story of an Irishman who was **crossing a stream** with mare and colt when finding it deeper than expected, and falling off the old mare. He seized the colt's tail in reaching the shore. Some persons on the bank called to him, advising him to take hold of the mare's tail, as she was ablest to bring him out. His reply was that it was a very unseasonable time for **swapping horses**."

The American Masonic Register and Literary Companion, however, had previously carried this tale on April 4th, 1840.

For an exhaustive study of the origins and evolution of this proverb and its use in other countries see *The Folklore Historian, Volume 24*, 2007, published by Indiana State University.

Perhaps the most famous horse proverb is **You can lead a horse to water, but you can't make it drink**." This is a very old proverb in the English language, and is still in popular use after all of these centuries. It was recorded as early as 1175 in *Old English Homilies*.

"Hwa is thet mei thet **hors** wettrien the him self nule **drink**en? (Who can give water to the horse that will not drink of its own accord?)"

Its implied meaning goes for people—they will only do what they have a mind to do.

Hoofing it is a slang expression for walking, taken from horses which have hooves. The earliest verifiable citation of 'hoofing it' comes in *The Temple Bar, a London Magazine, for town and country readers*, conducted by George Augustus Sala, July, 1862, in 'The Strange Adventures of Captain Dangerous' on page 11:

"The Keepers were always on our track; and sometimes the Sheriff would call out the Posse Comitatis, and he and half the beef-fed tenant-farmers of the country-side would come horsing and **hoofing it** about the glades to catch us."

ing mention of horses whatsoever:

> "With such **hoofing it** we may be sore, feel feeble too, towards dusk;
> Our light fare may even oft recall the Prodigal's dry husk.
> Then, perhaps, like Medes of old, I walk as if the end I'd greet;
> For dismounted, as you know, they found too tender were their feet."

From the early 1920s it has also been used for dancing. In **Babbitt**, on page 359, Sinclair Lewis used it this way:

> "Personally I don't see a whole lot of difference. In both cases they're trying to get away from themselves — most everybody is, these days, I guess. And I'd certainly get a whole lot more out of **hoofing it** in a good lively dance, even in some dive,.."

Hold your horses, meaning 'hold on' or 'wait,' was taken from pulling back on the reigns of a horse to bring it to a halt. Of 19 century American origin, the earliest citation of a form of it is from the New Orleans newspaper, **Picayune** in September, 1844:

> "Oh, **hold your hosses**, Squire. There's no use gettin' riled, no how."

Horseracing is one of the most ancient sports in the world, with nomadic tribesmen of Central Asia racing since early domestication of the horse around 6,000 years ago. In England, it can be traced back to the 12th century, after the knights returned from the Crusades with Arabian horses. The first horse racetrack was laid out on Long Island in 1665, but the sport did not become popular in America until after the American Civil War in 1868, when the American Stud Book was started. **No horse in this race,** however, is not old at all. It is a modern figurative expression used by someone to state that he or she has no vested interest in, or will not be affected by the outcome of something, while it is sometimes used in the converse form for the opposite. It is now common around the world in English speaking countries. The earliest citation of the phrase appears to be a *Boston Globe* article on August 10, 1994 by Alex Beam titled *'Can Dogs Paw Their Way Back to the Top?'* which doesn't seem to clearly indicate the metaphoric meaning, though it is close, and may actually have been the first printed example of a phrase which could have already been in oral use. Here is the snippet:

"But I have **no horse in this race**. I own a cat and a dog. The cat is named Einstein, because he is a genius."

But this from *The Federal Raid on Ruby Ridge ID: Hearings before the Subcommittee on Terrorism...U.S. Senate, 101st Session,* September and October, 1995, in quotes, may have been picked up from Beam's article, and makes the metaphor shine through:

"Nonetheless, I agreed to the interview and was assured by the FBI agents involved they have **'no horse in this race'** and are committed to a fair and factual investigation."

The term **dark horse** came from the same logical circle—the racetrack. A dark horse was one of obscure origins which few people felt had a chance of winning a race. The term is usually applied after a 'miracle' alters fate. Later it caught on, like other animal phrases, and was applied to people.

The earliest known reference was from Benjamin Disraeli in *The Young Duke*, 1831.

"A **dark horse**, which had never been thought of ... rushed past the grand stand in sweeping triumph."

The figurative usage of the exact phrase seems to have first been applied to academia in 1865 in Sir Leslie Stephen's *Sketches from Cambridge by a Don*.

"Every now and then a **dark horse** is heard of, who is supposed to have done wonders at some obscure small college."

There is one more metaphor which can be traced back to horseracing. **The old grey mare ain't what she used to be** has come to mean that some particular person is growing old and but a shadow of his or her former self. It is from a traditional folk song which is believed to have been based upon the extraordinary performance of 'Lady Suffolk,' the first horse recorded as trotting a mile in less than two and a half minutes. This transpired on 4 July 1843 at the Beacon Course racetrack in Hoboken, New Jersey, when the mare was more than ten years old. The lyrics to the song begin:

"Oh, **the old gray mare, she ain't what she used to be**,
Ain't what she used to be, ain't what she used to be.
The old gray mare, she ain't what she used to be,
Many long years ago."

Speculation as to the author includes Stephen Foster, but is uncertain.

Old warhorse has come to mean a variety of things depending on who's talking. It can be an old standard well-loved play or piece of music which has lost its luster in the modern age; it may also apply to a retired person, often military, who was highly respected.

As far back as the 17th century, a warhorse was originally a vigilant charger employed by a gallant knight which dashed valiantly into battle. Later it was applied to a cavalryman. The following is from a journal published in June, 1887 titled *The Nation, Volume 44, Number 1146:*

"The theatre of the war which broke out in 1653 between England and Holland, then at the height of her ... was the first land; to a son of the Anglo Saxon race, it was the old home. ... He had bestridden the **war-horse** to good purpose ..."

During the American Civil War, in the 1860s, Confederate Commander, General Robert E. Lee greeted his close friend, General James Longstreet, calling him, 'my old war horse.' Afterward, 'War Horse' became Longstreet's nickname.

This likely catapulted the term into popular usage as we know it.

Horse sense means common sense or good judgment in making practical decisions. The term is most often claimed to have been originated in the American West in the mid-to-late 19th century and is supposed to be based on the belief that horses are smart and have good instincts, though this idea is disputed by some. This was not the earliest coining of the expression, however. That actually goes to British romance novelist Evelyn Malcolm, in *Forsaken; Love's Battle for Heart*, published in *The London Story Paper*, in January, 1805, referring to a rough and tough young man:

"Lud, Bill Perkins has **horse sense**."

It is likely that the idea conveyed unsophisticated, yet basic, common sense of many uneducated people in that era.

Forms of **Beating a dead horse** have been used in English since the mid-19th century. It means to keep 'harping' on an issue which has already been resolved. It was originally 'flogging.'

The origin may most aptly be revealed in *The Fireside, Annual* published in London in 1877 by Rev. Charles Bullock:

"The man that was on his way, with a friend, to "Islington, N.," had heard many a time and again the allegory about **flogging a**

dead horse, but here was the very sign and symbol, fact and parable, experience and moral."

And down a bit in the text the allegory is stated:

"Here was this nearly **dead horse**, and there was this stupid and cruel flagellator trying to whip it up into standing posture, **to flog it** back into life and power."

It had appeared in *Watchman and Wesleyan Advertiser* newspaper in London in 1859.

"It was notorious that Mr. Bright was dissatisfied with his winter reform campaign and rumor said that he had given up his effort with the exclamation that it was like **flogging a dead horse**."

Some horse metaphors seem to have nothing to do with horses. A **charley horse**, for instance, is a sudden knot to swell up on a leg or arm, and may be caused by a knuckle-pounding. Actually, the term came from a horse kick. *The Doctor's Book of Home Remedies II*, 1995, says, **"This out-of-the-blue leg cramp is as intense as a kick from a palomino."**

The earliest printed reference located is from January 1904 in *The Outlook Magazine, Volume 76*:

"A **charley horse** guard interprets itself as a peculiar stiff, padded guard of the large frontal muscle of the thigh, which is very amenable to the deep 'charley horse' bruise, so called — tricksy players in earlier football epochs..."

Another odd expression is **Horse feathers**! What could horses possibly have to do with feathers? Originally a single word, this term was coined in the U.S. in the late-1920s as a euphemism for horses**t by cartoonists. It was used by T. A. Dugan, who often went by TAD, as evidenced in a 1927 annotated dictionary of his clever work, *A TAD Lexicon*, published by etymologist Leonard

Zwilling. Then Billy de Beck, creator of *Barney Google* cartoons, assumed credit in the December, 1928 issue of the journal, *American Speech*.

The changing of the term to two words was accomplished in 1932 in the Marx Brothers film by that name.

This is also used to express disbelief.

Some may have believed that **a horse of a different color** was coined in the classic movie, *Wizard of Oz* in 1939. However, the origin of this thought goes all the way back to 1601; Shakespeare in *Twelfth Night, II, iii.*

"My purpose is, indeed, **a horse of that color.**"

Although this referred to something being of the same matter, rather than a different one, the 'stage was set' and by the end of the 18th century, the 'tables were turned,' and it began being used to denote the opposite. For example, in 1798, an article in *The Philadelphia Aurora* used the phrase of President John Adams, sarcastically dubbing him King John I in comparison to the monarch of England, King James I.

"Whether any of them may be induced… to enter into the pay of King John I is **a horse of another color.**"

Grinning like a horse eating briars is an old Southern American expression which means smiling broadly and showing lots of teeth. It goes back to at least the 1880s. The earliest known citation is referring to a horse. It appeared in a Monroe, Louisiana newspaper, *The Ouchita Telegraph*, page 4, column 2, 16 July, 1887:

"Keren is brewing some sack for the fond father, when up comes Mister Peter Mouldy with his knitting and **grins** at her across the caldron **after the fashion of a horse eating briars.**"

A children's story by Rudyard Kipling titled 'Old Man Kangaroo,' first published in 1897, and later in *Harper's Magazine, Just So Stories*, and other books, used a similar line, "Grinning like a horse-collar."

As is common with many old sayings, this one has been modified through the years. Later printed examples from the early 20th century and forward more often used jackass or mule, and what they were eating ranged from sawbriars to cockleburs and thistles.

In spite of the statement made by noted journalist, Barry Popik in his popular column, "The Big Apple," August 9, 2013, that the earliest example of this was in *Butcher Bird*, a novel by Reuben Davis, 1936, an earlier citation appeared in the 1931 University of Arkansas, Fayetteville yearbook, *Razerback,* on page 145:

> "Captain Pickrin grabbed some unfortunate opponent around the neck and carried him out the front door and down a flight of steps and came back in **grinning like a jackass eating briars.**"

Don't look a gift horse in the mouth is a proverb which comes from the fact that by examining a horse's mouth, a person who is trained to do so can determine their age. Their teeth project a bit more forward each year. This phrase means 'don't examine too carefully the motives of a person who is making a gift to you without asking for something in return, or try to examine its worth before accepting it gratefully.'

This ancient saying is of obscure origin and goes back to at least the 16th century. The first known printing of a similar proverb was 'Don't look a given horse in the mouth' in John Heywood's 1546 work, *A dialogue conteinyng a number in effect of all the prouerbes in the Englishe tongue.*

> "No man ought to **looke a geuen hors in the mouth.**"

Heywood's work is the source of early printings of many sayings. He was employed in the court of King Henry VIII and Mary I as a musician and playwright. His proverbs rank only second to those of the *Bible* in historic significance, it seems.

One-horse town is an old metaphor for a very small, unremarkable town which is usually regarded as dull and boring. Originating in the 18th century, the expression 'one-horse' referred to a buggy or plow which was drawn by only one horse. It began to be used figuratively by the mid-19th century. It was cited as early as 1853 in an Oregon newspaper to describe a small 'one horse' meeting. Charles Dickens explained the use of 'one horse' to refer to not only a town, but other mundane entities in it in his magazine, *All Year Round* on February 18,1871, in an article titled, 'Popular American Phrases':

"'One horse;' an agricultural phrase, applied to anything small or insignificant, or to any inconsiderable or contemptible person: as a '**one-horse town**,' a 'one-horse bank,' a 'one-horse hotel,' a 'one-horse lawyer.'"

Actually I could have included this one in the section about man's best friend, since that is the way it was first used in print, as best I can tell. **I've got to see a man about a horse** (or **dog**) is a euphemistic saying derived from the days when someone was going to settle a bet on a horse or dog race. Though now archaic, through the years it came to be used as a way to conceal what a person was actually leaving to do, such as going to the restroom or to purchase an alcoholic beverage.

The earliest known citation is in Dion Boucicault's 1866 play, *Flying Scud*, in which a character dances around a situation by saying:

"Excuse me Mr. Quail, I can't stop; **I've got to see a man about a dog**."

Other similar euphemisms have evolved in later decades, such as I'm going to see Mrs. Jones, or even the President.

Most horses are pretty good sized animals! **I'm so hungry I could eat a horse** is a very old hyperbolic colloquialism and means that a person is extremely hungry. It is not meant to be disgusting. It is like saying 'I am starving!' There are alternatives to horse, in other cultures; such as in France, a wolf, or in Spain, a bull. It means almost anything that is put before me, and a lot of it. In spite of the *O.E.D.* claim that this dates only back to 1927, Tobias Smollett who may have coined it, used the saying in Chapter XIV of *The Adventures of Sir Launcelot Greaves* first published in the monthly paper, The British Magazine in 1760, beginning in January.

> "I should feel heart-whole, if so be as yow would throw the noorse a'ter .he bottles, and the 'pothecary a'ter the noorse, and oorder me a pound of chops for my dinner, for **I be so hoongry, I could eat a horse** behind the saddle."

A horsewhip is a long leather whip use for driving and controlling horses. **Ought to be horsewhipped** is a hyperbolic expression used to mean that something someone has done deserves severe punishment. The saying goes back to the 19th century. An early citation appears in the 1842 autobiographical, self-published *Sketch of Elizabeth T. Stone* who was wrongly confined to a mental hospital in Belmont, Massachusetts, page 15:

> "About 4 o'clock in the afternoon Dr. Wheelock Graves came in to see me, and sat about ten minutes and conversed mostly with my sister about Mr. Miller, saying that he **ought to be horsewhipped** or put in prison."

Stalking horse, as a metaphor, refers to a person or entity that tests a concept or mounts a challenge with someone on behalf of an anonymous third party. In politics, it is a candidate who runs in order to provoke the election and allow a stronger candidate to come forward. The term originally derived from hunting wild foul, in which the birds were known to ignore the presence of horses and cattle. Hunters would cautiously approach their prey walking beside their horses, lurking behind them until the flock was within firing range. The animals trained for this were known as stalking horses. Surprisingly, the figurative use of the term dates to the mid-17th century. The earliest known citation is from *Relations and observations historical and political upon the Parliament begun Ano Dom. 1640*, a book including an Appendix Touching the Proceedings against the Independent Faction in Scotland, published in 1648, page 17:

"Let us no longer make Religion a *stalking-horse*; God, who is all Wisdome and all Truth, will not be deceived. If we talk like Christians, and walk like Turkes, Christ will not own us."

Metaphorically speaking, a **Trojan horse** is anything that is used to mask the truth in order to trick or harm an enemy. The earliest known figurative use in print is in William Drummond's *The History of Scotland, from the year 1423 until the year 1542*, published in 1655, page 248:

"…they directed me to ravage and plunder the more peaceable neighbours about; this **Trojan Horse** laboured to give me a command over Horses. All which imployments being contrary to my education…"

Literally, this is a tale from Ancient Greek Mythology. A large wooden horse was constructed by Epeius, a master Greek carpenter and pugilist. During the Trojan War (traditionally 1194 BC to 1184 BC) the Greeks presented it to the Trojans, pretending it to be a goodwill offering to Athena, goddess of War. The horse was filled with soldiers, who, once inside the impregnable city of Troy, came out that night, opened the gate, and let in their army who conquered their unsuspecting foe.

The expression, **Wild horses couldn't drag me away** is found in an original Rolling Stones song called "Wild Horses" written by Mick Jagger and Keith Richards, released on their "Sticky Fingers" album in 1971. But in spite of many reporting this as its origin, the term, derived from the fact that wild horses are strong and dangerous, and can pull with great strength and resolve, was in use a full century earlier. The first citation of a form of the expression is from *The London Journal*, October 7, 1871, in a serial titled 'Lady Thornhurst's Daughter' by Mrs. Harriot Lewis, Chapter 18:

"I would die for you, my lady, as you know, and **wild horses couldn't** draw from me a secret of your ladyship's."

Then, in 1883, in Edward King's *The Gentle Savage*, on page 54 we find:

"**Wild horses couldn't drag him away** from that piano."

A wink's as good as a nod to a blind horse is a proverbial saying originated in England by the 18ᵗʰ century. It means that for someone who is ready and able to understand something, any subtle signal will be sufficient. It usually is said of something thought off color or possibly illegal. The earliest citations are slightly different. The first one is from the play *Scottish Volunteers*, a farce performed first in 1745:

"LOVES: Where are you going; —what will you say when you're there?

"THOM: I'm not there yet.—

"LOVES: Do you mind what I say to you.

"THOM: Let me alone for that, **a nod's as good as a wink to dead horse**.

"LOVES: A **blind horse** you mean, you beast!"

In *The Egotist: or, Sacred Scroll*, 1798, it is attributed to Milton:

"I do not say they had better not – but I say nothing! – '*a* **nod** *is* *as* **good** *as* **a** **wink** *to* *a* **blind** **horse**' as Milton beautifully expresses it."

As time went on, 'a nod is as good as a wink' was most often reversed, and other things were used for horse (mule, man). Eventually it was mostly used without the ending all together.

The remaining expressions in this group have reference to the names of other members of the Equidae family.

Pony up as a metaphor, had nothing to do with ponies. It likely originated in America in the early 19th century, but was from English roots. It means 'pay up' and was usually applied to a bill which was overdue, or expected to be 'cash on the barrelhead.' The earliest known use in print is from the May, 1819 edition of *The Rural Magazine,* Connecticut publication:

"The afternoon, before the evening, the favoured gentlemen are walking rapidly into the merchant-tailors shops, and very slowly out, unless they **ponied up** the Spanish (meaning the money)."

The 1859 Second Edition, enlarged, of *Dictionary of Americanisms*, put out by John Russell Bartlett, page 332, has this explicit definition:

"To **Pony up**. A vulgar phrase, meaning to pay over money. Ex. 'Come, Mr. Brown, **pony up** that account;' that is, pay over the money."

It also gives us a hint as to an earlier version which obviously led to this saying:

"Grose gives a phrase similar to it: '**Post the pony**,' i. e. lay down the money."

'Grose' referred to Englishman Francis Grose who published the well-known *Dictionary of the Vulgar Tongue,* first in 1785; then

When Pigs Fly

in 1811; at that time, vulgar referred to colloquialisms, not obscenities. *The Slang Dictionary, Etymological, Historical and Anecdotal, a New Edition*, 1873, entry on page 258, sheds a bit more light on the original British origin of 'pony' in this sense:

> "Also a generic term for money. Post, to pay down; ' *POST the pony*' signifies to place the stakes played for on the table."

In British English, **talk the hind legs off a donkey** is a term which represents the height of persuasive ability. It means that a person can chatter endlessly without stopping or becoming boring. The story has been told that expression originated in Ireland and is a literal translation of the Gaelic phrase actually meaning 'make a donkey sit down on its rear end,' a very rare feat. If a person can achieve this impossible feat by talking, they are an extraordinary and influential orator. It is a bit uncertain if the Gaelic origin is true. The following is from *The Alpine Journal*, May, 1887, in 'The Ascent of Tetnuld Tau' by Clinton Dent:

> "In addition to the customary halts—about every quarter of an hour—for conversation, innumerable other delays were occasioned. Three or four times the small donkey was flattened down by his burden, and his little legs spread out sideways, so that he looked like a tortoise. This disaster, as might be supposed, set up much chatter; as if they thought that because they could **talk the hind legs off a jackass**, they could talk them on again. Then, all assisting, we propped the donkey up."

There is one slightly earlier citation in print, however, from *The Chaplin of the Fleet: A Novel*, Volume 1, by Sir Walter Besnant and James Rice, 1881, page 92:

> "'I believe,' said Mrs. Gambit, 'that this man would **talk the hind legs off a donkey**. Keep close to me, Miss Kitty. Here may be villainy; and if there is, there's one at least that shall feel the weight of my ten nails.'"

76

The final two have to do with mules. Notoriously these are common in the Southern U.S. where farmers over the past centuries used them to plow their fields. For over 100 years, every April in Columbia, Tennessee, Mule Day is celebrated with a parade, camping, vendors and special events. It actually lasts from Friday through Sunday. The event draws visitors from near and far to the "Mule Capitol of the World!"

Don't kick a pullin' mule is a Southern Americanism used by Jack Daniel Distillery in Lynchburg, Tennessee, to illustrate the importance of keeping something that aids the area where it is. Another old Southern saying explains the reasoning behind this, **'When a mule is kicking, he is not pulling, and when he's pulling, he is not kicking.'**

He has enough money to burn a wet mule, another an old Southern American saying, is from the 1880s. Through the years it has often been used in negative political confrontations, particularly when referring to someone with a large sum of disposable funds, especially when the money may have been obtained dishonestly. It was used in 1935 by Carleton Beals in a quote from a controversial Louisiana governor in *The Story of Huey P. Long*:

"Huey described the battle graphically. 'They have filled up the city with **enough money to burn a wet mule**... They are laying their plans to try to ruin me...'"

Cattle, Oxen, etc.

One of the most popular farm animals has always been cattle. Perhaps it's because both milk and beef come from them. For the dairy cow, giving up her milk is a contribution, but for the beef cattle, their contribution to our food supply is the supreme sacrifice. Though there are fewer metaphors about cattle than horses, there seem to be more about bulls than cows. The first one I will look at is "**Like a bull in a china shop**." This means that the actions of a person are overly clumsy and / or careless, insinuating that he or she would break fragile items easily. This simile has been in use since the early 19th century. Some claim that the earliest known citation is from Frederick Marryat's novel, *Jacob Faithful* in 1834, however, it had appeared in many publications years before. As early as 1811, in *Heads of the People: or, Portraits of the English*, in an essay titled "Tavern Heads," by Charles Whitehead, the following appeared:

"Wang Fong wouldn't much like John Bull to invite himself to tea in his territories; that would be **a bull in a china shop**, with a vengeance! we should pretty soon crack their canisters…"

Cock and bull story combines a farm fowl with the bull! This very old idiom is applied to a tale which seems so fanciful that it is entirely unbelievable to anyone who is not extremely naïve. The story has been well circulated that the phrase was coined at Stony Stratford in Milton Keynes, a market town in Buckinghamshire, England. The name Stony Stratford stood for 'the stony ford on the Roman Road' of Watling Street, now called the 5A. In the 18th and

19th centuries, at the height of the coaching era, this was a vital mail and passenger stop between London and the North of England. The Cock and Bull were two of the main inns in town, and rivalry between the guests frequenting the two establishments is claimed to have reached fever pitch, resulting in exaggerated fantastic tales, which became known as 'cock and bull stories'. Both inns still exist. This, however, is not the true origin of the phrase. Versions of it actually predate this period.

Old folk tales featured magical animals. The first actual citation in English of 'cock and bull' is from John Day's 1603 play, *Law Trickes*, Act IV, page 66:

"Didst marke what a **tale of a cock and a bull** he tolde my father whilst I made then and the rest away."

The early 17th century French term, from which this more likely derived, is *coq-a-l'âne*. Randle Cotgrave's *A Dictionary of the French and English Tongues*, 1611, referenced elsewhere in this book, listed the saying with the definition;

"An incoherent story passing from one subject to another."

The literal translation of the French is 'from rooster to jackass.' Later the Scots used this saying as 'cockalayne'. Another way of saying this is the term we in America have heard, 'cockamayme' (also spelled cockamamie). Either way, the meaning fits well with 'cock and bull.' Bull was being used as a term for silly stories even earlier.

Then in *The Anatomy of Melancholy* by Robert Burton, 1621:

"Some mens whole delight is, to take Tobacco, and drink all day long in a Tavern or Ale-house, to discourse, sing, jest, roar, talk of a **Cock and Bull** over a pot, &c."

Though a tavern is mentioned in the one above, the context of these citations do not jive with the story of the infamous British inns. A cock and bull indicated tales of farm denizens. Both hotels were there before the 17th century, but the story that the derivation of the phrase was from there was apparently not 'hatched up' until the 20th century, and seems a bit cockamamie.

Like "take the reins" and "take the bit between one's" teeth in the previous section, **take the bull by the horns** means to take charge of a difficult situation and bring it under submission and control. It has been speculated that it originated in Spain or America, and possibly derived from either bullrunning or Spanish bullfights in which the banderilleros aim darts into the necks of the bulls, then wave red cloaks and grab them by the horns to hold their heads down. The practice of grasping bulls by the horns continued in the early American West, and subsequently in rodeos and is known as 'bulldogging.'

However, in spite of another major reference work dating the first citation of this expression in English to 1873, it was in use seventy years earlier at the dawn of the 19th century, when we find a definition and explanation of the expression in *Arciologia of Miscellaneous Tracts Relating to Antiquity,* Society of Antiquaries of London, 1803:

"A proverb in use at the present day is grounded upon this ancient practice of signifying conquest by the capture of the horns. 'To **take the bull by the horns**,' is an equivalent phrase for '*to conquer.*' When Demetrius Phalereus was endeavouring to persuade Philip, the father of Perseus, king of Macedon, to make himself master of the cities of Ithome and Acrocorinthus, as a necessary step to the conquest of Peloponnosus, he is reported to have used the following expression, 'Having caught hold of **both horns**, you will possess the **ox itself**.'"

The reference given was an ancient Greek manuscript Strabo, Lib. VIII, page 361. Strabo (64/63 BC – c. 24 AD) was a Greek philosopher and historian, and this refers to book 8 of his famed seventeen-volume *Geographcia*. Demetrius Phalereus, (Greek: c.

350 BC – c. 280 BC), to whom the original phrase was ascribed, was an Athenian orator.

Like a red rag to a bull has reference to a deliberate provocation intended to bring about an adverse effect. As early as the 17th century, 'red rag' meant someone's tongue, and waving it meant constant prattle. In *The Classic Dictionary of the Vulgar Tongue* by Francis Grose, 1785, he listed this saying:

"Shut your potatoe trap, and give your **redrag** a holiday."

The earliest mention in print of using a literal red rag with creatures is form *A Rich Cabinet with a Variety of Inventions* collected by "J.W." printed in London in 1668. Here it is catching a duck:

"Presently he getteth about a yard of strong thread, and .finding a little **rag** of **red** cloath, tyeth it to one end of the thiead, and at the other end tyeth a piece of Cheese (some what lesser than a Bean) with part of the rind on, and throweth it amongst the parings to the Fowle."

Then in 1724, there was in reference to trapping a pheasant with a red rag in John Trenchard and John Gordon's religious essays, *Cato's Letters:*

"Foxes are trapann'd (*trapped*) by Traces, Pheasants by **a red Rag**, and other Birds by a Whistle; and the same is true of Mankind."

After that references were made to other critters such as snakes (to extract venom) and turkeys, but bulls were not recorded as being attracted by red cloths until March, 1836, when the first figurative use of the term appeared in *Tait's Edinburgh Magazine* in 'Sam Pogson's Jealousy':

"'Consarn them red coarts!' was Samuel's first exclamation; — 'they catch wimmin's eyes **like a red rag at a bull**.'"

Bulls, however, cannot distinguish color, so the use of red in bull fights is for the advantage of the human audience rather than to distract the bull, who would react the same to any cloth waved before his eyes.

Bull dust is a euphemistic Aussie slang expression for rubbish or nonsense, which equates to the similar Americanism. It may also be applied to a fine red dust found in the desert regions of Australia. Use of this term in that country dates to the 1920s. The earliest available citation is from *Register News-Pictorial*, Adelaide, South Australia, December 7, 1929:

> "Motoring across Lake Eyre ... This **'bull' dust** might be about two feet deep, and cakes on the surface, so that it is hard to penetrate."

A bum steer is a piece of false information, whether given on purpose or not. Actually, it is attributed to 19th century American maritime humor. 'Steer' in this connotation does not actually refer to male cattle, but rather to steering a ship in reverse.

It is currently admittedly used more in Australia and New Zealand, but in spite of claims by other researchers that it had only been known in America since the 1920s, *The Foundry*, a publication printed in Cleveland, Ohio, in the issue for April, 1901, has the following in the feature 'Chimmie Powers Answers to Correspondents,' on page 18 in an entry by S.E. Attle:
> "Give de gaffer a **bum steer** de first chanst yu get."

Over the next several years it was cited in numerous U.S. publications including the *Anamosa Prison Press*, Anamosa, Iowa; Saturday, October 24, 1903:

"Somebody's been giving the P. P. man a **bum steer**."

Then, in the *Saturday Evening Post*, April 22, 1905 in 'A Meteorological Misadventure,' a humorous story by Kenneth Harris on page 7:

"I studied on it as we plowed along through the dust, and I couldn't help thinking that the Professor had got what is technically known as a **bum steer**."

American citations over the next few decades seem limitless and it was mentioned in *The American Language* by Henry Louis Mencken, first published in 1919, in the 1936 edition.

"Bum as an adjective (as in **bum steer** and bum food), bum's-rush"

Previous researchers appear to be more accurate as to its appearance in the U.K. around the end of World War II.

Now for the female gender of the species. The term **cash cow** was brought back to Britain from India by soldiers who noticed the natives in India offering money to temple idols in the form of sacred cows. It was coined in its present meaning in the 1960s by management guru, Peter F. Drucker.

Normally, a cash cow product has high market share in a slow-growing market, and is responsible for a large amount of the company's profit.

In 1977 *BPC Banker's Magazine, Ltd*, Volume 221 included the following on page 27:

"Two recent mergers indicate the problems in growth markets with a high rate of inflation and without **a cash cow** to support them."

The term is also used in sarcasm by sales and business persons to describe customers who have no control over their spending habits.

Though it seems likely that **holy cow** also was derived from the sacred cattle in India, It actually was first known to be used by baseball players as early as 1913, and likely much earlier by American baseball broadcasters. It is believed to have been coined by Halsey Hall, an announcer in Minneapolis, Minnesota from 1919 to 1977.

How now brown cow? is a rhyming phrase sometimes said jovially as a greeting. It was originally used in elocution teaching to demonstrate rounded vowel sounds. Each 'ow' sound represents the diphthong /au/ in the International Phonetic Association's phonetic alphabet. Use of this phrase dates back to at least January 1, 1926 when it appeared in *Elocution Do's and Don'ts* by Louie Bagley.

By 1942 it was being used in jest. It was cited in the Maryland newspaper, *The Capital*, in February that year:

> "Laird Cregar, now contributing his booming voice to 'Ten Gentlemen from West Point,' explains how he got it. When first tried out for the Pasadena Community Playhouse his voice wouldn't carry past the front rows. Coach Belle Kennedy has him declaim **How Now, Brown Cow** and The Rain in Spain Still Stains over and over."

Brown Cow, as a term, however, goes back as far as the early 18th century, when it was in use in Scotland as a jocular name for a beer barrel. Alan Ramsey used it in *The Gentle Shepherd, A Scotts Pastoral Comedy*, in 1725:

> "The auld anes think it best With the **brown cow** to clear their een.

Milk something or someone (for all it's, he's or **she's worth)** is a figurative expression for attempting to get as much out of

84

something or someone as possible; take full advantage. Today it is believed to be from continuing to squeeze on a cow's udder until every drop of milk is extracted. There was first, however, an old legal term 'mulct.' The origin of this goes back as far as the early 16th century. David Hume, in his *History of England*, 1529, states that Parliament granted King Henry VIII a discharge of all debts, saying that his creditors 'were well pleased to **take the opportunity of mulching them.**' In the context it implies that they were getting back as much as they possibly could. Certainly this could be the origin of the current term 'milking them.'

Why buy a cow when you can get the milk for free? most often means 'why get married when you can have sex without that commitment?' but can be adapted to other examples. The origin is uncertain, but forms of it have been in use since at least the late 19th century, as observed by this reference found in Benjamin Orange Flower's *The Arena*, Volume 2, 1892, on page 362, in a novelette, '*The Shadow of the Noose*' by Ferdinand C. Valentine:

"My mother did not hesitate to openly declare that Aunt Helen had been deserted by numerous lovers because (to quote my mother) '**why should they buy a cow when milk** was so cheap?'"

Thirteen years later it appeared in current form, using 'free' on 16 October 1905, in the large Georgia newspaper, the *Atlanta Constitution*, page 7, column 4:

"Some claim that Hoke Smith does not control The Journal, and has no personal organ. He would be a fool to **buy a cow when milk is free**. Why should he want an interest in a paper that seems to place him on a pedestal of virtue unequaled since St. Paul?"

Note that this reference had nothing to do with marriage.

Now cows will take their time ambling back to the barn—unless they are dairy cows needing to be milked. But cattle in general were the premise of the saying, **"Till the cows come home,"** which has been with us since at least the early 19th century. The place of origin could have been Scotland. It first appeared in print in January, 1829 in *The Times*.

"If the Duke (of Wellington) will but do what he unquestionably can do, and propose a Catholic Bill with securities, he may be Minister, as they say in Scotland '**until the cows come home**.'"

In the 1933 film, *Duck Soup*, Groucho Marx, in his normal dry, straightfaced humor, made the statement:

"I could dance with you **till the cows come home**. Better still, I'll dance with the cows and you come home."

The saying seems no less popular today, and means for an undetermined, likely *lengthy* period of time.

Put out to pasture is a metaphor which makes senior citizens cringe. Looking back, the word pasture is from the Middle English, and derived from the Latin *pastura*, meaning 'grazing.' Cows or horses which are thought to be past the age to bare young, and, in the case of cattle, give milk, are put out to pasture, and sometimes sold for various purposes…food for carnivorous animals, dog food, etc.

This term, in a literal sense, was used as early as 1735 in *The Complete English Copyholder* (A guide to lords of manors, etc.) Volume 1, page 155:

"For this reason a horse, &c, **put out to pasture** by Way of agiftmant may be distrained."

In the 20th century, the term 'put out to pasture' gradually came to apply to humans who were past their productive years, and means 'forced to retire.' It is equally popular in both England and the U.S.

An early reference leading up to this is from *Billboard Magazine*, November 3, 1945, in an article about the end of American Tobacco subsidiary, Kay Kyser's 'lend-lease' to Colgate Palmolive by G.W. Hill on page 5:

"Hill let Kyser **out to pasture** at a time when cig manufacturers generally were putting in their horses…"

The metaphoric idiom **all hat and no cattle** means the same as "all bark and no bite," in the section on dogs. It implies that something is pretentious, lacking in substance, action or power. The earliest known printed reference is found in *Ural-Altaische Jahrbücher*, Volumes 51-53, page 87, 1979:

"As they say in Texas, **all hat and no cattle**. To be retained from those pages is just the proposal that the Yiddish verb base davn- could come from Kipchak — and that's not a fact but a suggestion."

A form of the saying is the title of a 1981 report by Harvard Business Review: *Big Hat, No Cattle; Managing Human Resources.*

Several publications of the middle 1980s state that this is a Texas saying. *The Regis Touch: Million Dollar Advice from America's Top Marketing Consultant*, by Regis McKenna on page 27 says:

"There's an old Texas saying about a cowboy who was '**all hat and no cattle**.' That is, he was all show and no substance."

The British also have a saying, "all froth and no substance."

The simile "**strong as an ox**" is centuries old and goes back to Old French, Old Greek and Old Latin. Its thoughts were passed down in folklore through the tale of Paul Bunyan, who was said to utilize a blue ox named Babe. Oxen have been used by many civilizations as a beast of burden because of their great size and strength. It would make sense to describe someone who was exceedingly stout as 'like an ox.'

The earliest printed reference known is from *The Scripture Chronology Demonstrated by Astronomical Calculations*, by Arthur Bedford, 1730, Book II, chapter XI, page 268:

> "Some think, that by the Ox and Hawk, they only meant the sun, who is **strong as an Ox**, or as *(q)* David saith, *as a giant to run his course.*"

Also domesticated are some types of buffalo and bison. Being **buffaloed** is a slang term for being confused, bluffed and / or intimidated. The use of buffalo as a verb goes back to the late 19th century, according to etymologists, to the American West. Early on it referred to hitting someone over the head with the butt of a pistol. Good printed examples in that context appeared several times in Alfred Henry Lewis' novel, *On Sunset Trail* published in 1906; this citation being on page 180:

> "When one is too great to be '**buffaloed**' he is free to the gun of any man he injures."

In 1917 we see the modern usage in *Wilt Thou Touchy* by Sewell Ford, on page 93:

> "I don't deny he had me **buffaloed** for a while there…"

Sheep & Goats

We have already examined feline metaphors. But taking a look at the expression **black sheep**, we need to step back a bit. Black cats are traditionally a symbol of bad luck, and beware the chance that one may cross your path! Black was associated with mourning as early as the 2nd century in Rome, something likely adapted from the ancient Egyptian culture. *Bête noire* is French for "black beast" and means something disliked or feared.

In the *Bible* (*Psalms 23:1, 100:3*), people were depicted as sheep, and the Lord as the shepherd. In pre-industrial times, black sheep were less valuable than white ones. Perhaps this was caused by the idea of black being associated with evil or the devil. As a result, a 'black sheep' in a family became a term applied to a less-desirable member.

Some other sheep metaphors originated in the *Bible*. **Like a lamb to the slaughter** means a person has been 'sacrificed' for a cause. It is taken from the Bible and referred to the sacrificial death of Christ. It is found both in the Testaments. In *Isaiah 53:7*:

"He was oppressed and he was afflicted, yet he did not open his mouth; **like a lamb that is led to slaughter**, and like a sheep that is silent, so he opened not his mouth." *(ESV)*

Then in *Acts 8:32*, when 'the eunuch' was reading the verses from Isaiah.

Sacrificial lamb, as a metaphor, refers to someone or something that is given to authorities for the purpose of being harmed or destroyed for the common good. It is derived from the Old Testament religious practice of sacrificing a lamb which is a highly valued possession. *Exodus 12:5* states the requirements under the Law for a sacrificial lamb:

"Your **lamb** shall be without blemish, a male a year old. You may take it from the sheep or from the goats," *(English Standard Version*)

In Christianity, Jesus is pictured as the final sacrificial lamb, as we see in *I Peter 1:19, NIV:*

"but with the precious blood of Christ, a **lamb** without blemish or defect."

In politics, this term 'sacrificial lamb candidate' is applied to a candidate who is used to contest an election with the foreknowledge that he or she has almost no chance of winning. This meaning is historically recent, and a good example is found in Robert Hardin's 2007 novel, *Paradise Marred*:

"They have you losing less than five points from your almost thirty point lead over the **sacrificial lamb** candidate the Republicans put up against you."

Two shakes of a lamb's tail is an idiomatic expression for 'with lightening speed.' It is derived from how quickly sheep twitch their tales. The earliest reference in print is found in *Ingoldsby Legends* by Richard Barham, 1840. But it wasn't until a bit later when it became popular in magazines and novels. In *Hunt's Yachting Magazine*, February 1, 1868, we find:

"…we had no time to spare, as the tide was falling fast, and out we tumbled, and in '**two shakes of a lamb's tail**,' we were under way and got outside with but six inches of water under our keel."

The quotes indicate that the phrase was in use, but was likely still unfamiliar to many readers.

A wolf in sheep's clothing also originated in the Bible This descriptive metaphor for a person who appears to be a friend, but is in truth a foe, comes from *Matthew 7:15* (*NIV*):

"Beware of false prophets which come to you in **sheep's clothing**, but inwardly they are ravening **wolves**."

Shakespeare used a form of it in *Henry VI Part I (I,3,53-55):*

"Winchester goose! I cry, a rope! A rope!—
Now beat them hence; why do you let them stay?—
Thee I'll chase hence, thou **wolf in sheep's array!**"

Mutton dressed as lamb is a derogatory British idiom used to refer to an older woman who is dressed in a style more compatible to a younger woman. It has been in use in Great Britain since early in the 19th century. Just before the advent of the term, butchers were offering mutton dressed like venison, as seen in *The Housekeeper's Instructor, or Universal Family Cook*, by W.A. Henderson, London, 1805, page 461:

"Haunch of **Mutton dressed like** Venison"

The idea of mutton being dressed in a way different than what was normal likely inspired the term. It was first put in print in 1811 by Mrs. Frances Calvert in a social gossip journal then related 100 years later in a dialogue involving Mrs. Calvert and her husband in Knox Blake's *An Irish Beauty of the Regency*, on page 177:

"Girl!' answered he, 'Girls are not to my taste. I don't like lamb; **but mutton dressed like lamb**!'"

As a boy growing up on a farm we raised a lot of goats. I loved caring for them. But traditionally goats "got a bad rap." An **old goat**, figuratively speaking, applies to an elderly man who is commonly disliked. One who is hateful or disapproving of younger men and boys. The term was popularized in old western movies, television shows and comic books. Thomas E. Watson, however, used the term before this in his shocking book, *What Goes on in Nunneries? And Is Your Brain for Sale*, 1918, page 14:

> "Is there a difference in principle between the wretched street-walker and the girl who sells herself to a wealthy **old goat**— covering the sale with an elaborate marriage ceremony?

Getting someone's goat is getting up their 'ire.' To discover the origin of this, a little American book, written under the pseudonym, "Number 1500" published in 1904, *Life in Sing Sing* has the answer. In it, the word 'goat' is given as slang for anger.

The first mention of the phrase, per se, seems to be from a Wisconsin newspaper called *The Stevens Point Daily Journal* in May of 1909.

> "Wouldn't that **get your goat**? We'd been transferring the same water all night from the tub to the bowl and back again."

It made its way to England by at least 1924, when it was used in a story by Nobel Prize winner John Galsworthy called *White Monkey*, clearly seen as a recently coined expression.

> "That had **got** the chairman's **goat**! – **Got his goat**? What expressions they used nowadays!"

As a part of that 'bad rap' goats are seen as lacking in common sense. **Doesn't have the sense God gave a billy goat** is a Southern Americanism which evolved in the late 20th century from similar sarcastic insulting metaphors. An early example of this type phrase is in the writing of famed *Atlanta Constitution* humor columnist, Louis Grizzard, and is found in *Won't You Come Home, Billy Bob Bailey*? 1980.

"This is a free country, and if somebody **ain't got the good sense God gave a** sweet potato, it ain't up to me to move ... Otherwise, you'll have lumps, and you don't want lumps. Salt and pepper and stir in enough butter to choke a **goat**."

Note the slightly later reference to a goat. Eight years later, Chapel Hill, North Carolina writer, Nancy Tilly included the following in her juvenile novel, *Golden Girl:*

"But Penny felt as left out sitting next to Jack's sister as she had with Henry. There Tracey was, with the girls who dated football players. If I had **the sense God gave a billy goat**, I'da joined the Pep Club and be sitting with Tracey…"

Could talk the horns off a billy goat is also a 'Southernism,' or expression native to the Southern United States, and particularly in Texas. But it's only one of many of these. Other related sayings include "Freeze the horns off a billy goat," "Worry the horns off a billy goat," and "Preach the horns off a billy goat."

The earliest available citation to as expression involving a billy goat's horns, however, is in James Frank Dobie's Texas Folklore Society publication, *Rainbow in the Morning*, 1926, page 84:

"It's cold enough to freeze **the horns off a billy goat**."

In 1989, this citation of 'talk the horns off' appeared in *Sat Success* by Joan D. Carris, William R. McQuade and Michael R. Crystal on page 201 in 'Fun with Modern Idioms':

"**talk the horns off a billy goat**"

Farm Fowl & Domesticated Birds

This group encompasses such feathered friends as chickens, ducks, geese, turkeys, and peafowl. We don't have any guineas, but they fit here too! Then we have canaries and parrots which live in luxury with their humans. Some which include entries from another category are covered in those sections.

Let's start with the bird which supplies us with a lot of breakfast comfort in the form of eggs and made Colonel Sanders famous. This is another domesticated creature which has gotten a bad name! **Chicken-livered** is a common metaphor which means easily frightened, timid, fearful or cowardly. It derives from the fact that chickens are easily spooked and run at the slightest noise. The first example we have of 'chicken' meaning a coward comes in 1595 in *An Humble Supplication to Her Maistie* on pages 22 and 23:

> "John Savage, likewise when he came vnto the Court, was soe well knowne to be **a Chicken** of that fether, that two Pinsioners were charged to have a spetiall eye on him, and to watch him soe long as he stayed there…"

The first mention of 'chicken-livered' as a separate idiom was in the British novel, *Old Bachelors, Their Varieties Characters and Conditions* (by the Author of *Old Maids*) 1835, page 103-104:

> "Talk of a hen-pecked husband, forsooth! — a wife's authority may be excused or tolerated, as in nine cases out of ten, she

governs for the benefit of her family and her faint-hearted spouse: but the authority of a housekeeper — the hen-pecked Old Bachelor! — truly this is pushed to extremities that would make the veriest **chicken-livered** husband in existence rebel."

Hen-pecked, cited in the above 1835 text, had its origins in the practice of a female chicken pecking about to show their dominance over another hen. This also gave birth to another expression, **pecking order**.

This is a colloquialism for a hierarchical system of social organization first described by Norwegian zoologist Thorleif Schjelderup-Ebbe in 1921 in his PHD dissertation. Originally under the German terms *Hackordnung* or *Hackliste,* it was introduced into English in 1927. The initial use of the term referred to dominance in chickens asserted by various behaviors including pecking as a means to measure leadership order, especially between males and females, which was extended to other species of fowls (and animals) as described in ***Bird Display: An Introduction to the Study of Bird Psychology*** by Edward Allworthy Armstrong, 1942, page 171:

"THE SOCIAL HIERARCHY IN BIRD LIFE Social hierarchy amongst birds and animals — Various types of dominance — Peck-dominance and peck-right — **Pecking-order** between male and female — Mitigation of despotism amongst strongly social birds…"

By the late 1960s, it had begun to be applied to the hierarchy within a social group or community of people in which those at the top assume positions of leadership, authority and power. One of the first such citations known is from ***Social Theory and Social Structure*** by Robert King Merton, 1968, page 249:

"Formality is manifested by means of a more or less complicated social ritual which symbolizes and supports the **pecking order** of the various offices."

Madder than a wet hen is a popular simile which is difficult to pin down for origin, but it is likely that this originated in the Southern Appalachians. It is common mountain belief that chickens get angry when they are dumped into a tub of water. When Southerners use this phrase, they mean that someone is as irate as one can imagine.

Play chicken is the colloquial name originally given to a dangerous game of dare made popular in the 1950s in which two cars race toward one another. The first one to pull away from the collision course is 'chicken,' or coward. The term, however, has since come to be used in a figurative sense to political and economic challenges, even going so far as the threat of nuclear war.

Along the lines of dominance among these fowl is the term **Rule the roost**. The word 'roost' is from the Middle English of the eleventh century, and 'ruling the roost' has been said of 'roosters,' a common term for a male chicken, for hundreds of years. It is used metaphorically for a person who dominates a family or group of people. A similar metaphor would be '**cocky**,' which is derived from the other word for a rooster. The phrase, however, is not restricted by gender, but can be a female family member who 'wears the pants.'

The expression originated in the 16th century in a bit different light. The first known version is from English poet John Skelton in *Why Come ye not to Courte* (published c. 1550), line 198:

"He **ruleth all the roste**."

Elizabethan playwright and author, Thomas Heywood, in *Gunaikeion* (a poetic history of women), page 286, in 1624, recorded it this way:

"Her that **ruled the rost** in the kitchen…"

Then John Heywood in his 1546 book of proverbs, part i chapter iv:

"**Rule the roast.**"

Shakespeare also had this in *Henry VI Part 2* (1:1) 1596-1599:

"The new-made duke that **rules the roast**..."

It wasn't until the mid-17th century that 'roost,' per se, began to also be used, and by the 20th century, displaced roast altogether.

While we're on the subject of roosting, **Curses come home to roost** is a saying which comes, in this exact form, from Margaret Mitchell's *Gone With the Wind*, 1936. But as a proverbial expression, the thought is over 600 years old. The fuller form was 'Curses are like chickens, they always come home to roost.' It was used to express the fact that one's offensive words or actions are likely to come back to them at some point. This appeared in *Roughing it in the Bush, Or. Life in Canada* by Susanna Moodie, 1852:

> "The nest time the old woman commences her reprobate conduct, tell her to hold her tongue, and mind her own business, for **curses, like chickens, come home to roost.**"

The idea, however, goes back to Chaucer in *The Parson's Tale*, circa 1390 in which he said curses are "**like a bird that returns again to its own nest.**"

Lay an egg is not a term which originated with chickens, as one may think. In the early days of playing cricket, it was determined that 'a duck's egg' meant you had no runs. No score was a zero, which looked a lot like an egg. Now we use the term 'goose egg' to mean zero. Today the term 'lay an egg' signifies failure. Again lending to the negative image of domesticated birds.

Chicken scratches is an idiomatic expression, ignored by other phrase dictionaries, which has been in use since at least the mid-20th century, when it began to be used by school teachers to describe incredibly poor handwriting of some students. It is derived from the fact that when fowls scratch in the dirt they produce odd markings. Usually only the writer can interpret what is meant by these scribbles. It may also be the derivation of the term 'scratch paper' used for doodling.

Just chicken feed is used to mean a paltry sum, especially in regard to money, and often in contrast with a larger amount. The earliest known citation is from *Life Magazine*, October 27, 1941, on page 39 in an article titled "A. F. of L. Ditches a Racketeer but Cannot Ditch its Critics":

> "The misdeeds of Mr. Browne and his kind may cost the U. S. public millions of dollars, but this is **just chicken feed** to Thurman Arnold (right), head of the Department of Justice's anti-trust division."

The practice of placing eggs into hens' nests to encourage their laying more was recorded in print as early as the 14th century. Figurative use of the term **nest egg** to refer to savings has been around since at least 1686. In 1927, Locke & Clarke published a collection of letters bearing that date including the following:

> "The rest, I perceive, he is not troubled should remain as a **nest egg** till a farther occasion."

Which came first, the chicken or the egg? is the quandary debate that still rages today between creationists and evolutionists. The following quote from Aristotle (384-322 BC) originally came to us from François de Salignac de La Mothe Fénelon's *Abrégé des vies des anciens philosophes*, published in Paris, 1726, page 314. This translated version comes from *Lives of the ancient philosophers*, published in London, 1825, page 202.

"If there has been a first man he must have been born without father or mother – which is repugnant to nature. For there could not have been a first egg to give a beginning to birds, or there should have been a first bird which gave a beginning to eggs; for a bird comes from an egg."

And still on the subject of eggs, **Don't count your chickens before they are hatched** is a tidbit of wisdom which is one of the oldest of this type of sayings. It was first recorded in Aesop's fable from 570 BC entitled *The Milkmaid and Her Pail*.

"'Ah, my child,' said the mother, '**do not count your chickens before they are hatched**.'"

It was much later used by Thomas Howell in *New Sonnets and Pretty Pamphlets* in 1570. Obvious is the intent—don't be so quick to count on something that may not materialize, particularly financial gain.

"**Counte not thy Chickens that vnhatched be**, Waye wordes as winde, till thou finde certaintee."

A little later there is a reference used by Samuel Butler in his narrative poem, *Hudibras* in 1664.

"To swallow gudgeons ere they're catch'd, And **count their chickens ere they're hatched**."

Hatched up figuratively has come to mean invent a plan, usually erroneously, to accomplish something of one's own desire and making. It comes from hatching eggs to raise chickens or other fowl, and is native to the Appalachian region in the Southern U.S. The following is the earliest known reference in print, and comes from the September, 1888 issue of *The Century Illustrated Magazine* in a story titled 'The Mountaineers about Monteagle':

"But 'thout a pertendin' ur a lettin'on ter counterdick 'em, I thes up an 'lowed ter the feller ez hed done the main chance er the praincin' roun,' how 't them all was mighty fine p'ints fer showin' off an like's not they growed naiterlez chinkipins whur that cuntrivance wus **hatched up**, but how ez I'd hyern tell 't outsiders had ter do some monsturs tall tradin' afore they'd git a hold er 'em."

In past centuries, chickens were often killed by chopping their heads off with an ax. They are, however, not able to even walk after their heads are removed. Their nerves do jerk a bit though. Running around **like a chicken with its head cut off** is a figurative phrase which was known in the United States as early as the late 19th century, and appeared in print as a simile by the 1880s. It means so busy that one hardly knows what is going on. It was used in an article about an escaped prisoner in *The Atlanta Constitution* in July of 1882.

> "Finding himself free from the heavy shackles, he bounced to his feet and commenced darting about **like a chicken with its head cut off...**"

If a rooster crows after sundown, he will get up with a wet head is an old superstition from folklore. A book by Fletcher Bascom Dresslar, 1907, *Superstition and Education* from the University of California at Berkley includes it this way:

> **"If a rooster crows when he goes to bed,**
> **He's sure to get up with a very wet head."**

A whistling woman and a crowing hen always come to no good end is another comical old folk saying which has been phrased many ways over the past 160 plus years—it is likely much more ancient. The earliest known reference in print is from *Notes and Queries: A Medium of Inter Communication for Literary Men, Artists, Antiquaries, Genealogists, Etc.* (Edinburgh, Scotland,

1851), page 164, and is from the printing of the paper on August 10, 1850:

"A whistling woman and a crowing hen,
Is neither fit for God nor men."

It is herein called, 'an old proverb often quoted in this district.' Since then, versions include a bragging woman and various endings, but the one in the above quote seems likely to be the original, as it appears in a number of older citations. One 1871 source (*The Yorkshire Magazine, Volume 1*) states that the crowing of a hen was taken as a sign of evil or a token of death in a family. Several sources mention a similar French proverb.

Flew the coop is American slang for 'ran away.' Often now it is merely used when someone leaves home. It is derived from chickens flying out of a coop to avoid impending danger. Foxes and hawks are a very real threat to poultry. Now caged fowls usually are totally enclosed to prevent this disaster, though other threats often take their tolls. It has been in use as an idiom since the late 19th century. Used here as a dialect expression, an early example is from Frank Leslie's popular New York *American Magazine* in a story by Victor Speer titled "Vision in Baxter Bay," December, 1893:

"She didn say dat we wuz dead skins, an dat she wuz tipped off for heaven, but she jes come right out in de middle of de room an sez: 'Men, wo all kicks over de traces an **flies de coop** sometimes, but de Boss is alius ready ter take us back.'"

Then in 1900, it was listed in the American Dialect Society's *Dialect Notes*:

"fly the coop, v. phr. To leave suddenly; to run away. 'He got in debt to everybody and then flew the coop.'"

No spring chicken, as an idiom, was first recorded in 1906 in *The Encyclopedia of Word and Phrase Origins*.

One story is that in the early days of settling New England, chicken farmers discovered quickly that chickens born in the spring brought a better price in the fall than older chickens which had gone through even one winter. Occasionally a farmer would try to pass off an older chicken for one born that spring. Upon examination, the buyers would remark, "That's no spring chicken!"

The phrase caught on and has long been used to apply metaphorically to people who have passed their prime.

As rare as hen's teeth, 'as scarce as hen's teeth,' and 'scarcer than hen's teeth,' are similes used to mean that something is non-existent. Chickens, on the whole, don't possess teeth at all, and digest their food by first collecting it in their craw, a sack which gradually releases the food to their 'second stomach,' called a gizzard, which serves as a grinder of a sort.

However, it was reported in *Science Daily* on February 26, 2006, that scientists have discovered a breed of chicken called Talpid that actually has a complete set of choppers. Interestingly enough, there is a team of researchers, based in the Universities of Manchester and Wisconsin, that have actually developed a process which can induce growth of teeth in normal chickens.

The actual origin of this simile, however, is very obscure, but it goes back to at least the mid-19th century and likely earlier. *The Richard H. Adams, Jr. papers*, U.S. Civil War records of 1862, has a notation at the bottom, "Records of the 5th Cavalry are **as rare as hen's teeth**." This seems to be the earliest reference in print.

The earliest known reference in print to the American slang expression "**beat a hen a-pecking / a-rootin**', referring to something highly unusual, is in the *Winchester Journal*, an Indiana newspaper, on October 25, 1876:

"Peter Reinheimer thought it **beat a hen a-pecking**."

The hen a-rootin' version, which prevailed throughout the 1950s in the South, was first attested in 1939, according to The University of Wisconsin-Madison's *Dictionary of Regional English*.

Chick, as slang for a young woman, according to *Etymonline*, the online etymology dictionary, is first documented in 1927, in Sinclair Lewis' *Elmer Gentry*, supposedly from American black slang.

Ain't nobody here but us chickens is a saying which was long popular but has faded into oblivion. Most people who used it in the 1950s and 1960s likely thought, and it was often stated, that this saying, and the derivative, '**just us chickens**,' came from the 1946 popular song by this title recorded by Louis Jordon and His Tympany Five, written by Alex Kramer and Joan Whitley Kramer. Actually, the saying is quite a bit older. A reader submitted joke in in the July 19, 1908 issue of *Everybody's Magazine* about a chicken thief caught in the act had thief making the statement:

"'Deed, sah, dey **ain't nobody hyah 'ceptin' us chickens**."

And finally, **Winner, winner, chicken dinner** is an old expression which is used in fun when someone has won something. Legend has it that it originated as a result of the fact that many years ago every casino in Las Vegas had a three piece chicken dinner with a potato and another side for $1.79. A standard bet back in those days, goes the legend, was $2, hence when you won a bet you had enough for a chicken dinner. So, the victory cry became "Winner, winner, chicken dinner!" This entire tale is difficult to prove.

The crude 2008 movie, *21*, and ESPN color analyst, Randy Petersson, actually popularized the phrase in modern days. In the film it was said to have originated at Binion's Horseshoe Casino in Las Vegas, now a Harrah's property. The narration by an unseen male while cards fly across the screen in the opening scene is:

"'**Winner, winner, chicken dinner**.' Those words had been dancing around my head all night. I mean, it's Vegas lore, that phrase. Just ask any of the old-time pit bosses, they'll know. It was a Chinese dealer at Binion's who was first credited with the line. He would shout it every time he dealt blackjack. That was over 40 years ago, and the words still catch. '**Winner, winner, chicken dinner**.' There it is! '**Winner, winner, chicken dinner**.'"

Binion's actually did serve a 10 ounce New York strip steak for $2.00, however, according to *The St. Louis* (MO) *Herald*, 27 March 1994, in the article "No such thing as free lunch—says who?" by Carolyn Olson, Travel, page 2T:

"A 10-ounce New York strip steak with salad and baked potato for $2 at Binion's Horseshoe from 10 p.m. to 5:45 a.m."

But the Chinese blackjack dealer likely picked the phrase up from an earlier source. David Guzman, co-author of *A Guide to Craps Lingo from Snake Eyes to Muleteeth*, revealed in an email:

"'**Winner Winner Chicken Dinner**' came from alley craps back in the Depression. They used to play craps in alleys and didn't always use $$$, but if they did it use $$$ and they were winning, it meant they could afford chicken for dinner that night."

Guzman feels that the saying may have had its roots in Cockney rhyming slang.

Another story is that in the late 1960s and early 1970s at trap league 'meat shoots' in Waseca, Minnesota, teams of sportsmen would compete by shooting at flying clay pigeons. The winners would take home a frozen chicken. The announcer would call out, "Winner, winner, chicken dinner!" Again, the earlier origin could have caused them to use this line.

Next we turn toward our web footed friends, ducks and geese.

Though this seems like merely a statement of common sense, **If it walks like a duck, swims like a duck, and quacks like a duck then it probably is a duck** is used to let people know that they need to exercise a bit of good judgment when dealing with persons who exhibit characteristics which are typical of charlatans or other undesirable characters.

American poet, James Whitcomb Riley (1849–1916), coined this comical phrase when he wrote, "When I see a bird that **walks like a duck and swims like a duck and quacks like a duck, I call that bird a duck.**"

Later Riley's quote was popularized by Richard Cunningham Patterson, Jr., the U.S. Ambassador to Guatemala, in 1950, during what was commonly called 'the cold war.' He accused Guzman's government of being Communistic, stating:

"Suppose you see a bird walking around in a farm yard. This bird has no label that says 'duck.' But the bird certainly **looks like a duck**. Also, he goes to the pond and you notice that he **swims like a duck**. Then he opens his beak and **quacks like a duck**. Well, by this time you have probably reached the conclusion **that the bird is a duck**, whether he's wearing a label or not."

This became known as the 'duck test' and was used in 1964 by Cardinal Richard Cushing in regard to Fidel Castro.

While we are looking at phrases made popular in politics, **lame duck** is a metaphoric expression which refers to any person or thing which is now unable to perform properly, especially one which was previously able to do so. It is most often applied to politicians who are in their final term in office, and even more likely to be used when the current office-holder has just lost an election. The original meaning, however, had to do with the Stock Market in London and refered to investors who were unable to pay their debts. The earliest known citation is from Horace Walpole's *Letters to Sir Horace Mann*, 1761:

"Do you know what a Bull and a Bear and a **Lame Duck** are?"

A Selection of Leading Cases on Various Branches of the Law, 1855, makes the meaning clear:

"He is a **lame duck**,' meaning that he was incapable of fulfilling his contracts…"

Then in a few years later, though still used in the previous manner we see the present meaning come into play in *The Congressional Globe* entry for January 14, 1863:

"In no event could it be justly obnoxious to the charge of being a receptacle of '**lame ducks**' or broken down politicians."

Historically, **dead duck** has also been used in the U.S. as well as in the U.K. and Ireland. These terms both were dreamed up in the same era. 1829 seems to be the applicable year that 'dead duck' was brought to light on both sides of the pond. Early that year *The New Monthly Magazine* printed this attributed to John Bull:

"CXCII. A **dead duck** is not a duck in law, after Judge Littledale; a dead rabbit is a rabbit, after Judge Burroughs; sheep are not sheep if any of them are rams, nor horses horses if any of them are mares: — such is the law;…"

On May 15, *The Glasgow Herald* reported that the following was first in the *Glasgow Morning Register*:

"In opposition to the dictum of Judge Littledale, that a **dead duck** was **not** a duck, Mr. Serjeant Adams has decided that a dead rabbit *is* a rabbit. The vitality of a duck is one vitality, and the vitality of a rabbit is another vitality."

Whatever paper first reported this; it seems to have been aimed as a political arrow at the said Judge and possibly began the term to apply in that manner. One month later, the *New York Currier* printed this:

"There is an old saying 'never waste powder on a **dead duck**;' but we cannot avoid flashing away a few grains upon an old friend, Henry Clay."

Without doubt, this quip was aimed at Clay. Then a letter to the Editor of the *Hartford Courant* (Connecticut), on August 29, 1839 describes accusations made by another party with regards to the next General Election by saying:

"Respecting this accusation, he let off his popgun at the **dead duck.**"

Obviously, by this time the definition was established.

Like a duck to water, usually preceded by takes to (something), is a simile which speaks of someone having a natural tendency or talent toward a particular field of endeavor or subject, and enjoying 'diving into it' immensely, even the first time it is approached. The earliest known reference to it in print is from the July, 1860 issue of *Baily's Magazine of Sports and Pastimes* in 'Our Jockeys:'

"…he took to a horse **like a duck to water.**"

The metaphoric saying **like water off a duck's back** has been in popular culture since at least the late 19th century and derived from the fact that ducks have oily feathers. When rain falls, or they are doused all over with water; even when they have been in a pond, lake or river for hours and waddle ashore, the water not only runs off, but they appear totally dry.

The first printed reference known is from 23 May 1874 in *The Grey River Angus* reporting on a serious situation existing in Nelson, New Zealand regarding the Provincial Council and the government-owned Brunner Mine. Here is a clip containing the idiom:

> "This is one of the advantages of a non-responsible Government — that it can afford to allow hostile motions to glide **like water off a duck's back,** or rather like a pellet from the scales of an alligator."

In 1893 another article appeared in a New Zealand newspaper using the phrase. Then on 25 September 1894, the first reference known in an American publication was printed in the *Lawrence Daily Journal* in Kansas, in an ad for Pearline Soap placed by James Pyle.

> **"Like water off a duck's back** – so dirt leaves, when Pearline gets after it. No matter where it is, the easiest, safest, quickest and cheapest way to get rid of it is with Pearline. Washing clothes is Pearline's most important work."

This term can refer to anything intended to cause adverse effects, but which the victim ignored and allowed to have no effect.

When ducks light on a pond or lake they are usually away from any protection and thus are easy targets for hunters. A **sitting duck**, figuratively, is someone who has left himself or herself open to criticism or adverse action from his or her enemies. It started being used in this way in World War II, as in this early example from an article on page 4 of *Boys' Life*, October, 1944, titled 'Danger in the Air' by Richards Bennett:

> "Randolph knew that the general had been right when he had said he would be a '**sitting-duck**' for any Jap plane."

Alluding to the sound of a squawking duck in the death throws, **dying duck fit** is a metaphor for a loud demonstration of anger and frustration. Though having merely a 'duck fit' is known in the U.K., and someone looking like 'a dying duck in a thunderstorm' has been expressed in Australia, this saying is primarily used the Southern U.S. It is similar to a 'hissy fit,' but more violent.

Determining the origin is very difficult, but it has been in common use since at least the early 20th century and likely much longer. It is very likely that it came to the South as merely 'duck fit' with early Scots-Irish and English immigrants, and evolved in the Southern Appalachian slang.

Someone who blossoms from a less-than-handsome youngster into a near-perfect specimen of humanity as he or she matures is often dubbed an **ugly duckling**. It is taken from Danish storyteller Hans Christian Anderson's (1805 – 1875) most popular fairy tale by this curious title. The beloved tale, which Anderson devoted a year in development, was first published November 11, 1843, and has been translated into more languages than any of his other stories, and adapted to a musical and film. It centers around a youngling hatched in a nest by a mother duck which was much different from its mates. It was considered gangly and unattractive, thus received much verbal battering. After leaving the barnyard and finding a new home, then heading out on his own, the ugly duckling sees a flock of migrating wild swans and wants to join them. Being too young to swim, he takes up with a farmer for the winter. The next spring, the swans once again arrive and light on a pond near him. Now fully grown, he decides to join them, even though they may reject him and kill him because he is so ugly. The swans, however, welcome him into their flock, because he looks just like them. After all, he was really a swan all along. Anderson later admitted that the story was an analogy on his own life.

Quack is a slang term for an untrained person who pretends to be a doctor and gives medical advice and dispenses treatment. Though it would seem to derive from the noise made by ducks, according to author and etymologist, Matt Soniack, it is actually a shortened form of the Old Dutch world, *quicksalver,* spelled *kwakzalver* in modern Dutch. It originally meant a person who uses home remedies to cure sickness, later coming to mean one who uses false cures. The earliest form in Dutch, *quacsalven,* meaning home remedies, goes all the way back to the 1300s. The oldest known reference in print of 'quack' being used for a charlatan is in *Hieroglyphikes of the Life of Man* by Francis Quarles, 1638:

"**Quack**, leave thy trade; thy dealings are not right, thou tak'st our weighty gold, to give us light."

When it comes to geese, there are not so many.

Two well-known sayings seem to be linked together: **Your goose is cooked** and **Don't kill the goose that lays the golden eggs**.

Your goose is cooked means that a person has done something that he or she will sorely regret. All hope is gone, and that person is now in deep trouble.

One theory of the very early origin of this saying is that in the denizens of a besieged city in the 16th century hung out a goose to show their attackers that they were not starving. This so enraged the enemy that they burned the town and cooked the goose.

Another belief is that it referred to the 'goose that laid the golden eggs,' which the farmer killed to get the gold inside. Hence, the saying, '**don't kill the goose that lays the golden eggs**,' meaning do not destroy the one thing that will continue to provide for your needs.

There were references to **gone goose** as early as 1830, meaning a person beyond hope. One such example that year was in a newspaper called *The Massachusetts Spy*, which printed the phrase, 'You are **a gone goose**, friend.'

It seemed that the idea of 'cooking someone's goose' was floating around by 1845. In a South Carolina newspaper, *The Southern Patriot*, on 22 February of that year, the following humorous article appeared:

"HOW TO COOK YOUR NEIGHBOR'S GOOSE.—Collar him, take a moderate sized stick, hickory will do, stir him up; apply offensive epithets; when he boils over with rage, continue dressing, baste sufficiently, and when he's properly served out, **his goose is cooked**."

Printed reference to this phrase in the sense we know it dates to England in a ballad published in London in 1851 bemoaning the Pope's appointment of Cardinal Wiseman as Archbishop of Westminster.

"If they come here we'll **cook their goose**, the Pope and Cardinal Wiseman."

What's sauce for the goose is sauce for the gander, also used with 'good,' rather than sauce, in the U.S. commonly means 'what is good for a woman, a man should be willing to do.'

The saying in this form goes back to at least 1704, when it was recorded in *Brown's New Maxims*. An earlier form not using the word 'sauce' was reportedly in use from 1579.

A **wild goose chase** is a hopeless quest, which those pursuing would much rather have been spared. This saying is one from William Shakespeare, who brought us so many of these clichés. It comes from *Romeo and Juliet*, 1592:

"Romeo: Switch and spurs, switch and spurs; or I'll cry a match.

"Mercutio: Nay, if thy wits run the **wild-goose chase**, I have done, or thou hast more of the **wild-goose** in one of thy wits than, I am sure, I have in my whole five."

The basic feeling here is that chasing a goose will likely end in frustration, since wild ones can rise to flight 'before you can say Jack Robinson.' In Shakespeare's day, however, this related to a race in which a number of horses followed a lead horse and mimicked wild geese in flight.

By 1811, *Grose's Dictionary of the Vulgar Tongue* defined the term in the sense we know it today.

"A tedious uncertain pursuit, like the **following** a flock of **wild geese**, who are remarkably shy."

In 1978 a British film starring Richard Burton, Roger Moore, Hardy Kruger and Richard Harris named *The Wild Geese* was released about Irish Mercenaries who embarked on a near-impossible mission, leaving Ireland to serve in various armies in Europe.

Wouldn't say boo to a goose is an old country proverb which started in England. Most country folk had or knew someone who raised geese. It has been said that saying boo to a goose is a symbol of intimidating them. The saying indicates that someone who wouldn't even dare intimidate a goose is a wimp. However, stirring up a goose can cause an attack by the threatened foul. Geese are well known for grabbing a person's flesh and causing quite a bit of pain.

But there is more to this saying that meets the eye. From the 1500s, figuratively, a goose has meant a simpleton. Saying 'boo' to a 'goose' was thought to be the least brave act a person could do; so, yes, the meaning is basically the same. The person incapable of this is extremely timid and 'afraid of his or her own shadow.'

The earliest known reference in print is from *The Humours of an Election, a Farce,* as Performed at the Theater Royal in Covent Garden by F. Pilon, Scene I, 1780:

"*Letit*...But surely, you can never think my booby cousin will cut any figure in the House of Commons.
Parma. Why not, why not, you satyrical baggage?
Lelit. He can't **say boo! to a goose.**"

Then we have turkeys! They don't have a stellar reputation either!

Walk turkey in the 19th century meant to strut or swagger. A **jive turkey** is a term coined in the 1970s in African American slang for a jerk or a person lacking in common sense. In short, metaphorically, a turkey has long been an undesirable 'chump.'

It's hard to soar with the eagles when you are surrounded by turkeys is a humorous proverbial statement which has been attributed to Tom Way. It is, however, a quote from Frank Capra's 1936 classic romantic comedy, *Mr. Deeds Goes to Town*, and was spoken by Longfellow Deeds played by Gary Cooper, in the film. It means that it is difficult to be an effective leader when your closest associates and co-workers are uncooperative. A 2002 remake featured Adam Sandler as Mr. Deeds.

Gobbledygook is a nonsensical expression which has reference to language that is meaningless or is made unintelligible by excessive use of abstruse technical terms. According to *Merriam Webster*, the first known use was in 1944. U.S. Congressman Murray Maverick of Texas disliked drawn out dialogue and rebelled against the pompous way in which information was being presented in Washington, coining this word to describe it, "based on the meaningless 'gobbling' noise of turkeys when made by human gook."

Though there are a variety of opinions by researchers on the origin of the phrase **talk turkey**, meaning 'talk frankly and get down to business,' the one which seems to make the most sense is that it began in Colonial America in dealings between the natives and the colonists. There were plenty of wild turkeys about and the natives were well-equipped and trained to hunt them. There is one complex tale which says that a colonist and a native went hunting and agreed to share their spoils equally. The spoils supposedly consisted of four crows and four turkeys. The colonist is said to have given a crow to the native and then taken a turkey for himself all the way through. The native's response was that the colonist only talked crow for him and talked turkey for himself. A brilliantly written book, *The Etymologicon*, by Mark Forsyth, tells the tale a little differently as one turkey and one buzzard, stating that it was a joke, but seemingly indicating that it spawned this cliché as well as **cold turkey**.

Before **cold turkey** meant quitting drugs without help, it referred to **talking cold turkey**. **Going cold turkey** came later. The first known reference to this meaning is from a newspaper in Canada, *The Daily Colonist*, in October 1921.

"Perhaps the most pitiful figures who have appeared before Dr. Carleton Simon are those who voluntarily surrender themselves. When they go before him, they [drug addicts] are given what is called the '**cold turkey**' treatment."

This analogy was made because during quick drug withdrawal the person's blood is forced to the inside organs making the skin appear white and giving the skin a goosebump-like appearance.

The word 'poor' has been around since 1200 AD, and Job is a biblical character. This expression **poor as Job's turkey** is credited to a Canadian judge and humorist named Thomas Halliburton (1796-1865), using the pseudonym Sam Slick, and appeared in the mid-19th century. He described Job's turkey as so poor he had only one brother, and so weak he had to lean against a fence in order to gobble.

The book of *Job* in the **Bible** is believed to be the oldest of biblical writings, even before there was such a thing as an Israelite. It is the tale of a wealthy man who was taunted by the devil with the permission of God. After he had everything taken away and was lying in ashes with boils all over him, he still had faith in the Supreme Being. He was used as an example of patience. To be 'poor as Job's turkey' indicated the lowest estate imaginable. Job, of course, would not have had a turkey, as they are native to North America.

But there is one barnyard fowl which has never had a derogatory reputation. Peacocks are the male peafowl, and the appearance of their strutting about to show off their bright iridescent fan-like tail plumage led to the feeling that they were 'proud.' The earliest reference to the saying **proud as a peacock** is from *The Reeve's Tale* the third story in *The Canterbury Tales* by Geoffrey Chaucer, circa 1395:

"As any **peacock** he was **proud** and gay."

Domesticated birds, however, are not limited to those kept on farms. **As sick as a parrot** is a British expression. A doctor in Liverpool stated that the phrase originated from 1926 when the previously obscure disease of bird psittacosis became a pandemic of clinical importance, involving humans in twelve countries with more than 800 cases. This could have popularized the simile in the 20th century. But actually, this doesn't seem to ring true. Here's why.

First, the thought is actually much older. It was first coined by the dramatist Aphra Behn in her 1681 comedy, *The False Count*, in which the maid Jacinta says of her mistress Julia (Iii1),

"Lord, Madam, you are **as melancholy as a sick Parrot**."

This simile is used to expresses a feeling of disappointment rather than one of nausea because of the meaning in the play and its reference to Julia, who is deprived of liberty by her jealous husband.

Still, it doesn't appear much in books. In 1975 the following was on page 13 of *Imprisoned Tongues* by Robert Roberts where an illiterate speaks of his inability to learn:

"It's knocked me **sick as a parrot.**"

The cat that ate the canary was covered earlier, but there is another expression about this joyful little bird. The modern idiomatic expression, **be a canary in a coal mine** means to be chosen as the individual in a company or group who acts as a test person to uncover a dangerous situation, thereby clearing the way for others. It is derived from the era in the late 19th and 20th centuries when miners took a caged canary into a coal mine to detect if there were dangerous levels of carbon monoxide in the mine, in which case, the canary would die. If the canary lived, it was then considered safe to send in miners. An early figurative example is found in *The Militarization of South African Politics* by Kenneth W Grundy, 1986, page 85:

"Although it may be Pretoria's policy to regard the homeland security forces as part of a collaborative regional defense system to fight together against the Marxist onslaught, their anticipated role may be little more than the **canary in the coal mine** — to signal to the SADF that larger-scale action must be taken to stem the tide of opposition to a homeland government..."

Quite a bit is said in various sections of this book about pigeons, and carriers are often used to deliver messages, so I'm including pigeon metaphors here. **Pigeon hole**, also spelled **pigeon-hole** or

pigeonhole is a term which has changed drastically through the ages in perceived meaning. In medieval times, pigeons were raised domestically for their meat. Pigeon holes were openings in walls or cotes in which they nested. By 1785, when the following reference appeared in *The Case of Christopher Atkinson, Esq.*, this term had come to be applied to compartments in desks and offices in which items were stored, because they resembled the pigeon cotes.

"The sale-notes of purchases for the Board were put upon a file, and those of what was bought towards the execution of what I had sold the Board, were put into a **pigeon hole** in his desk."

Then by the mid-to-late 19th century, pigeon hole was being used as a verb for classifying something, or setting a matter aside with intent to return to it later. An example is from *The Galaxy*, page 93, January, 1874:

"He belongs to a class who, if a certain combination of sounds or letters has been uttered by somebody, somewhere, at some time — no matter who, where, or when — pounce upon it, classify it, label it, and **pigeonhole** it for preservation..."

Most commonly, **stool pigeon** applies to a person acting as an informer. When the phrase was first coined, in the 1820s, in the United States, it referred to someone acting as a decoy to draw outlaws into a trap—and it still may be used that way. The earliest available citation comes from *The Telegraph*, published in New York City on Saturday June 20, 1825, on the first page, under the heading 'Anniversaries,' but it had nothing to do with criminals:

"Indeed this popular preacher, having been countenanced and caressed by the Presbyterians, appears to have sold himself to them for a tool, or rather a **stool-pigeon** to decoy other Methodists into the snare designed to entrap them for the benefit of the Presbyterian clergy."

Many dictionaries state that this derived from a pigeon which was nailed to a stool, or a stump, to be used as a decoy. There seems to be no evidence of this use in a dictionary until the late 19th century. It is believed by some that the origin actually goes to the etymology of the words. Stool, in this sense, however, likely came from the French *estale* which was applied to a pigeon used to entice a hawk into a net. This word appeared in French from the early 1600s, and by the end of the 1700s, according to etymologists, stool pigeon was being used for a person used as a decoy. 'Pigeon' is also applied to someone who allows himself to be swindled.

Section Two

The Jungle, Forest & Desert

Savage Cats

Let's kick off this section with the undisputed **King of the Jungle**!

King of the Jungle was the title of a 1933 movie starring Buster Crab in which a man is raised by lions, in contrast to the tales of *Tarzan* who was raised by apes. Lions, however, had been dubbed Kings of the Jungle since at least the 6th century BC when the phrase appeared in Aesop's Fables, *The Lion and the Mouse* and *The Donkey in the Lion's Skin*. The opening lines of the latter are:

"A donkey stumbled across a lion's skin and decided to put it on. 'I'll be **King of the Jungle** for a day.' He thought."

As brave as a lion is a simile which is self-explanatory. It was first known to be printed in 1790 in *The Haunted Tower, a Comic Opera in Three Acts* by James Cobb in Act III, Scene ii:

"Bar. Alarmed, my lord? ''hy, though I am naturally **as brave as a lion**, yet, I do not like to be taken thus by surprise; it is that which alarms me; and Sir Palamede, I am sure is at the bottom of this.'"

Lion hearted means exceptionally courageous or brave. A lionhearted person continually challenges himself or herself, pushing on toward becoming the best that he or she can be. One major online dictionary cites 1700-1710 as date of origin, while a major dictionary places this at 1616. This is much closer. The earliest reference now available in print is actually in *The History* *of Great Britaine Under Ye Conquests of Romans, Saxons, Danes and Normans*, dedicated 'To the Most High and Most Potent Monarch, Iames' (James), 1614, page 473:

"...which (though it were afterward punished by the Lawes) might seeme a presage, that this **Lion-hearted** King (as his by-name Ceur-de-Lion did import) should beea fpeciall destroier of the Enemies of our Sauiour."

This is, of course, in reference to Richard I, the Lionheart (1157-1199). The French equivalent was in print as early as 1553 in *Annales et Chroniques de France, depuis la destruction de Troye* ... (Annals and Chronicles of France During the Destruction of Troy).

"Antost apres le trefpas dudict roy Henry, qui fut l'anmil cent quatre vingts & neuf fut Roy d'Angleterre ledict Richard, sonsils, parauant Comte de Poitiers, qui fut surnommé *coeur de Lion*: lequel païsa & accorda auecques ...."

Qui fut surnommé **coeur de Lion** translates to 'who was nicknamed Lion Heart'.

The idiom **the lion's share** means the greater portion of anything. Like 'King of the Jungle,' it has its origin in a number of *Aesop's Fables*, in which the lion claimed the greatest portion of the spoils when hunting with other animals. Aesop is credited with several of our common idioms.

Throw someone to the lions is another ancient metaphor. This refers to causing someone to be in an extremely dangerous or precarious position for which he or she is totally unprepared. It is said to have came from the practice of Ancient Romans who threw Christians to the lions in the Coliseum. This practice, however, is actually much older, and was ordered by Persian King Darius for Daniel (c 605 BC-533 BC), a Hebrew in authority, on a trumped-up charge by the princes of the kingdom, as described in the biblical book of *Daniel, Chapter 6, verse 16 (KJV):*

"Then the king commanded, and they brought Daniel, and **cast him into the den of lions**. Now the king spake and said unto Daniel, Thy God whom thou servest continually, he will deliver thee."

And finally, "**If March comes in like a lion, it goes out like a lamb; if it comes in like a lamb, it goes out like a lion.**"

This is a very old proverbial saying going back to at least the early 18th century. The first known mention is on page 221 of Daniel De Foe's *The Complete English Tradesman, Volume II*, printed in London by Charles Rivington in 1727, where it is plain to see that the first, and most likely part was already known:

"This, therefore is not the Case; but my meaning is, that the Tradesman should not, as **the Month of March is said to do** sometimes, invert the Course of Things, and **coming in like a Lamb**, go out like a Lion."

Thomas Fuller, in *Gnomologia: Adagies and Proverbs; Wise Sentences and Witty Sayings, Ancient and Modern, Foreign and British*, published 5 years later in 1732, states this of March:

"**Comes in like a Lion, goes out like a Lamb.**"

A leopard cannot change its spots is a proverb which is easy to decipher. Someone is what they are by their intrinsic nature. They don't usually change. Although some people really *do* change, the point is generally well-taken. You shouldn't fall 'hook, line and sinker' for someone's claim that they have changed until you examine their motives, and until they prove themselves.

This is a biblical paraphrase, and is from *Jeremiah 13:23a*.

"Can the Ethiopian change his skin, or **the leopard his spots**?"

Cougar is a modern term for an older woman, usually over the age of 40, actively seeking romantic encounters or relationships with younger men. The origin of the term is debated, but thought to have started in Vancouver, British Columbia, Canada as a put-down for older women who frequent bars, who were willing to go home with whomever was left at the end of the night. It likely derived from the fact that cougars are often on the prowl at night seeking prey.

The cliché expression, **the law of the jungle**, means that every person must stand on his own, thus, anything goes; it relates to the 'survival if the fittest.' It comes from a poem in chapter two of Rudyard Kipling's classic novel, *The Jungle Book*, 1894:

"Now this is **the Law of the Jungle** -- as old and as true as the sky;

"And the Wolf that shall keep it may prosper, but the Wolf that shall break it must die

"As the creeper that girdles the tree-trunk the Law runneth forward and back

-- For the strength of the Pack is the Wolf, and the strength of the Wolf is the Pack."

𝒲𝒾𝓁𝒹 𝒞𝒶𝓃𝒾𝓃𝑒𝓈

This takes us to **the leader of the pack**. A 1964 pop single for the group Shangri-Las by this name, written by George Morton, Jeff Barry and Ellie Greenwich, popularized this term and gave it the metaphoric connotation which we know today: someone who is a charismatic leader of an organization, gang, club, etc. In a literal sense, it comes from the alpha male in a pack of wolves.

The common metaphor, **lone wolf**, had its origin with wolves which leave their pack and strike out on their own in search of prey. It is applied to humans who eschew association with the masses, and particularly to those with rabid agendas such as terrorists and assassins. In *The Poetic Melange, Volume II*, published in Edinburgh in 1828, a literal lone wolf is referenced in print:

"Midst the towers of thy Salem the **lone wolf** is howling,
O're the wrecks of thy Temple the wild Arab strays
'Mong the tombs of thy fathers the tiger is prowling,
As a dream we remember the fame of thy days.—"

Lone Wolf was once a popular Native American name. In *Sheridan's Troopers and Borders* by De Benneville Randolph Keim, 1885, page 157, we find one of several references in print about Native Americans by this name:

124

"After some parlay Santana and **Lone Wolf**, and a Comanche, joined the column."

Wolf whistle is a metaphoric expression used for a very high pitched double-noted (rising, falling) whistle made to show great admiration; most usually a male for an attractive female, now often found offensive by women. The term is taken from the sound of a hungry wolf hollering; hence, a woman-chasing man has become labeled as a 'wolf.' Earliest citations began in the late 1930s according to a major phrase origin dictionary, and became more common during World War II. The whistle was used by 'Blitz Wolf' in Tex Avery cartoons beginning in 1942.

A wolf in sheep's clothing is a descriptive metaphor for a person who appears to be a friend, but is, in truth, a foe; this biblical expression comes from *Matthew 7:15* (*NIV*):

"Beware of false prophets which come to you in **sheep's clothing**, but inwardly they are ravening **wolves**."

Shakespeare used a form of it in *Henry VI Part I (I,3,53-55):*

"Winchester goose! I cry, a rope! A rope!—
Now beat them hence; why do you let them stay?—
Thee I'll chase hence, thou **wolf in sheep's array!**"

Another one involving wild canines and helpless sheep is **Don't let the fox guard the henhouse**. This proverb means that a job should never be assigned to someone who will then be in a position to use it for personal gain or to repay a vendetta. It first appeared in the French '*La contre ligue*,' translated into English by John Wolfe (1589), and is similar to the Latin saying: 'Ovem lupo commitere' meaning 'to set a wolf to guard sheep.' The proverb was first printed in America by Arthur Guiterman in *A Poet's Proverbs* in 1924. It has been used in several similar forms.

Cry wolf, meaning to give a false alarm, is derived from one of Aesop's fables (210, Perry Index, sixth century BC) "*The Boy*

When Pigs Flyegment>

Who Cried Wolf." In the story, a shepherd boy repeatedly tricks residents of a nearby village into believing that a wolf is attacking his flock by hollering, "Wolf! Wolf!" Eventually they are wise to his deception, and when a wolf actually does attack, they do not respond and the flock is killed.

Crazy like a fox is an antonym of **crazy as a loon**, because someone who is crazy like a fox is not crazy at all, but very shrewd. The saying took root from the title of a book by American humorist, Sidney J. Perelman, first published in 1944.

Taken from the Old English, *fox-hol*, meaning a fox's den, **a foxhole** is a hole in the earth used by a soldier as a small fort for protection against enemy fire. The term was coined in the military during World War I. The first use in print was in a U.S. Army report in 1918 describing German soldiers "building a hole in the ground to give sufficient shelter…to one or two soldiers."

126

Primates

Getting back to the deep jungle, we will now discuss primate metaphors. Monkeys are pictured as being playful creatures. **Monkey around** refers to doing random, unplanned activities; spending time idly. The first known reference in print is from 1881, in *Dick's Reflections and Readings Number Twelve* by Dick Fitzgerald in 'The Language of the Rail' by Bill Nye, on page 117, which became a part of his novel, '*Forty Liars and Other Lies,*' page 31 in 1889:

> "Now you don't want to **monkey around** much, for if you don't loom up like six bits and go out on the tick, the old man'll give you a time check and the Oriental Grand Bounce…"

Monkey business means any playful, tricky or underhanded act or practical joke that would tend to offend another person. According to *Merriam Webster* it was first cited in 1852. An American 'screwball comedy' movie by this name was made 100 years later starring Cary Grant. Actually, the true origin of the term came from an earlier expression, 'monkeyshine' coined in 1832, meaning 'disrespectful behavior.' It was used by Minstrel entertainer Jim Crow in a song deriding African-American slaves. It evolved from an even earlier British slang term, 'monkey tricks.' The earliest verifiable reference in print for 'monkey business' is in *Peck's Bad Boy and His Pa* by George W. Peck in 1883, page 91:

> "…but we must remember that there must be no **monkey business** going on."

There are numerous examples in print in the late 1880s and 1890s. Three 'Bad Boy' movies were made from Peck's book series in 1921, 1934 and 1938.

More fun than a barrel of monkeys seems to have undergone a transformation in more recent years to a felicitous application, meaning 'not fun at all' similar to the old phrase 'like fun!' is a later version of earlier phrases, which literally meant 'extremely cleaver and loads of fun.' The earliest known citation of a version of it is from George Darley's dramatic play, *Thomas à Becket*, 1840:

"De Traci chatters **More than a cage of monkeys**: we must wait."

Then, nine years later, we find a reference in print which gets us nearer to the current version in *Harper's Bazaar* on 21 December 1889:

"My brother... says the American girls are perfectly fascinating... He says they are **more fun than a box of monkeys**."

Other variations followed including a bushel, bag and cartload of monkeys. Then in December of 1895, Willard C. Gore used 'barrel' in the University of Michigan student magazine, *The Inlander* in a collective definition of the term under 'Student Slang':

"**Barrel of monkeys**, or bushel of monkeys, to **have more fun than**, to have an exceedingly jolly time."

The figurative phrase **Monkey see, monkey do** means whatever one does, someone else will mimic. The earliest printed reference to it is from February, 1922. *Transactions of the Commonwealth Club of California*, San Francisco, printed the following explanation in Minutes of the Year 1921:

"Harry B. Reynolds argued on both sides to establish the celebrated psychologic law discovered by Pythagoras, 'Monkey see, monkey do.'"

The person mentioned here is ancient Ionian Greek philosopher, mathematician and religious movement founder Pythagoras of Samos (c. 570-495 BC). It seems that this had reference to child psychology in which parents teach children to imitate their actions.

Get the monkey off someone's back is an old colloquial expression for removing or solving a problem or situation that has been difficult or has made someone unhappy. It is most often used in reference to addictions.

In John Bunyan's classic, *Pilgrim's Progress* (1678), in the migration from Turmoil to the City of Light, there is an analogy of everyone having burdens clutching to their backs with "claw-like arms," which is a precursor of this saying.

Early on in the 1800s, the earliest citations appeared in books about piggy-backing monkeys. The first figurative reference to someone having a monkey on his back, however, was in *The Parterre of Poetry and Historical Romance: With Essays, Sketches and Anecdotes,* Volume Five, by Effingham Wilson, Junior, published in London in 1836, page 218, under the heading "The Philosophy of Fairs":

"The abridged retires from society with a monkey on his back, and bequeathing a cordial benediction to the author of this diabolical "Essay on Man.""

Back in the 19th century and early 20th century, organ-grinders would dress monkeys up with a little jacket when taking them out to raise money. A monkey suit came to be a term for a tuxedo because the wearer was often embarrassed to wear one and felt like a 'monkey.' A popular online dictionary lists 1885-1890 as the time of coining. It was originally being called 'monkey jacket' as early as the 1820-1830. A great mid-19th century example is found in *The Trial, of Albert W. Hicks for Piracy*, by Edward A. Johnson, published in 1860, page 64. Hicks was executed on Bedloe's Island, New York on July 13 that year.

> "I saw the prisoner on board in the forenoon, and again in the evening, I think he had a **monkey jacket** on;"

It is impossible to know exactly when the term morphed from 'jacket' to 'suit', but in keeping with the online source, the earliest available reference in print of 'monkey suit' is found on page 9 of Charlotte Mae Young's *Chantry House*, 1886:

> "Gooch had only to thrust her hand into the pocket of his **monkey suit** to convict him on the spot."

The comical expression **I'll be a monkey's uncle**! is derived from a slam against Darwin's theory of evolution. It has a similar meaning to 'I can't believe that!' Obviously it didn't come into being until after Charles Darwin's theory was published in *On the Origin of the Species* in 1859. The famous 'Scopes Monkey Trial' (The State of Tennessee V John Thomas Scopes) was held in 1925 in Dayton, Tennessee, when the high school biology teacher went on trial for teaching evolution in violation of Tennessee's Butler Act. Scopes was found not guilty. This trial inspired the movie, *Inherit the Wind*, starring Spencer Tracy, Frederick March and Gene Kelly, 1960.

If you pay peanuts, you get monkeys is a brainy saying meaning that if an employer isn't willing to pay very much, the persons who work for him or her are going to be poor workers who will deliver poor results. It is often credited to flamboyant European Industrialist and author, Sir James Goldsmith. The earliest citation of a form of this proverb, however, is from a classified ad for a sales person in the *New York Times*, February 16, 1953:

"ONLY **MONKEYS WORK FOR PEANUTS**, but YOU will be working and making BIG MONEY with US."

According to several normally reliable sources, though this citation was not found, the actual statement was made in *Director* by Leslie Coulthard, in speaking of directors' pay, August, 1966:

"Shareholders want the best available businessmen to lead the companies and recognize that you get what you pay for. **If you pay in peanuts, you must expect to get monkeys.**"

This was followed by two others who obviously 'borrowed' it in 1979.

Cheeky monkey is a slang expression still in use today by folks in the British Isles and Australia; it peaked in television and media offerings in the 1970s and 1980s. It is utilized to chide someone in a playful, good-natured fashion, though it also may be used dismissively. It was common on such comedy TV series as 'Doctor in the House,' 'Open All Hours' and 'Are You Being Served.' It has been used referring to men who made advances on ladies as well as to refer to rambunctious or mischievous children. The phrase is never used in America. The earliest known printed reference is from 1962 in *Granada Manchester's Plays*, in 'Independent Means' by Stanley Haughton, Act II, page 118:

"*Sam:...* [To Mac] Oh, bring in an extra cup, will you?
Mac: Aye, sir. Do you want one, Mr. Watling?
Watling: **Cheeky monkey**. I put the kettle on."

Go ape over is a hyperbolic expression that means to become violently emotional or extremely enthusiastic about something. It is, of course, derived from the high strung antics of primates. A major dictionary of idioms incorrectly states the 'second half of the 1900s' as the era of origin. Ape, used to mean 'imitate,' goes back at least to the 1630s, and 'playing ape,' even further. The actual expression, 'go ape,' was in use by January 1, 1942 when John

Button, as Franklin W. Dixon published the Hardy Boys mystery, *The Clue of the Broken Blade*:

"She's very beautiful, but we're not going to **go ape over** her."

Early in 1959, Neil Sedaka released a song on RCA titled *I Go Ape*, with only minor success in the U.S., but reaching number nine in the U.K.

Like ugly on an ape is the modern variant of one used by Margaret Mitchell in her classic novel, *Gone With the Wind*, "ugly as a hairless monkey." According to renowned etymologist William Safire in his column On Language, headed "Like Ugly on an Ape," in *New York Times Magazine*, October 30, 1988, the only two recorded uses of this expression at that time had been by George (H.W.) Bush. The first time, Safire stated, was on August 10, 1981, when quoted in a U.P.I. story datelined Meridian, Mississippi.

"The Vice President said Russia pounced on the neutron-bomb decision '**like ugly on ape**,' but the Soviet Union's reaction was 'thoroughly expected.'"

The second time was immediately before Safire wrote the column in 1988:

"I KNEW THE MINUTE I said 'card-carrying member of the A.C.L.U.,'" George Bush told Maureen Dowd of The New York Times, "a couple of your best columnists would jump all over me **like ugly on an ape**."

Even Safire could be mistaken, though. In the long-running TV Western, *Gunsmoke*, Season 10, Episode 4, "Crooked Mile," October 3, 1964, after Cyrus (George Kennedy) threatened to kill Quint (Burt Reynolds) unless he stayed away from his daughter (Katherine Ross), Festus (Ken Curtis) snaps at him, "If you do I'll get on to you **like ugly on an ape**!"

Elephants

We can't leave out these metaphors about the large jungle animal which may also be tamed and used as a beast of burden.

Elephant in the room is an idiom which refers to an obvious problem or truth that no one wants to talk about. It comes from the fact that if an elephant were in a room, it would be impossible for it to go unnoticed. To show how inaccurate some can get, Derek Paget, in *No Other Way to Tell It*, 1996, attributed the actual coining of phrase to Irish writer, Bernard MacLaverty:

> "Bernard MacLaverty was already a well known Irish writer when he took on the screenplay for *Hostages*…For example, his 1983 novel Cal was filmed in 1984 by David Puttnam's Enigma Company. He is also the likely originator of the popular phrase *'the elephant in the room.'* He used the idea of an elephant in a room in his 1978 children's book *A Man in Search of a Pet.*"

However, the saying had been around much longer. Even the *Oxford English Dictionary* got it wrong by attributing it to *The New York Times* article June 20, 1959 which said:

> "Financing schools has become a problem about equal to having **an elephant in the living room**. It's so big you just can't ignore it."

In 1814, Russian poet and fabulist Ivan Andreevich Krylov wrote a fable titled *The Inquisitive Man*. Its main character went to a museum and noticed the minutest of details, but failed to see an elephant. The proverb was born of this tale.

In 1915, *The Journal of Education*, Volume 37, page 288, published in London, had the following:

"Is there **an elephant in the class-room?**"

A white elephant is something that is costly to obtain or maintain and provides little benefit or value. The idea comes from the Burmese belief that albino elephants are sacred. In Burma, they can't be used for work and they must be cared for with great diligence.

Giving a white elephant as a gift, however, would be done only to someone considered an enemy. The idea behind this is that your enemy's wealth would eventually be erased with the funds required to provide for the sacred elephant.

Bears

Loaded for bear is a cliché meaning to be ready for whatever comes, even when anticipating a fight, or the worst case scenario, regarding the challenge at hand. It is derived from the old frontier days when barrel-loaded muskets were used for all sorts of game. When hunting bear, the woodsman knew to pack in a powerful amount of gunpowder before adding the metal shot. The earliest known printed reference to the figurative phrase is from the Masonic publication, ***Transactions of the Annual Convocation of the Grand Chapter of R.A. Masons*** (Michigan), 1881, page 107, and is rife with of figures of speech (Note period spellings):

"The report on Foreign Correspondence is the work of a veteran, but can not say now whether a neophyte could have wielded those sissors as ably as did the veteran chairman—fact is, Companion Innes is always '**loaded for bear**' when his game is nothing but chipmunck or prairie hen…"

The quotations represent the fact that the idiom was already known to some degree.

Being **mama bear about** (something) metaphorically usually refers to a mother or other female responsible for care of children being excessively protective of a child or children, but may also apply to any subject which someone viciously defends. It is taken from the fierceness of a mother bear when defending her cubs, and only came into popular usage in the 21st century. An early example in print of the alternative use is from ***Standing By: The Making of***

an American Military Family in a Time of War by Alison
Buckholtz, 2009:

"'That sound is part of our marriage,' she said, firmly. 'I
wouldn't give it up for anything.'
"'I get it,' I said. 'You're very **Mama Bear about** the Navy,
aren't you?'
"'It's just part of my coupon-cuttin,' Spam-eatin' self,' she
laughed, dipping a nacho."

Smarter than the average bear is a phrase from the popular
Hanna-Barbera cartoon character, Yogi Bear, and his little
sidekick, Boo-boo. Yogi, whose name was a takeoff on baseball
great, Yogi Berra, first appeared in 1958, when Berra was a top
Yankee Hall of Famer, and World Series champ. Yogi Bear had a
number of catchphrases in his vocabulary, the best known of which
is this one. He proclaimed himself 'smarter than the average bear,'
and sure enough, he was. Yogi was a talking bear who had no
problem with the English language. Now, the phrase is used to
describe someone who seems a notch above the crowd in
intelligence and /or ingenuity.

Dromedaries

Another popular beast of burden, particularly in the Sahara Desert, is the camel.

There is no doubt as to the definition of the old idiom, **the straw that broke the camel's back**. 'The last straw' and other such sayings are related, and mean that one problem after another has been piling up, and finally the entire weight of the situation was simply too much to bear. This phrase comes from an old Arabic proverb about a camel which is loaded to such a capacity that it is no longer able to stand under the burden.

Charles Dickens receives credit for one of the earliest printed figurative references to this in English in *Dombey and Son* published serially from 1846-1848.

"As the last **straw breaks the** laden **camel's back**…"

The phrase is used in many other languages including Spanish, French, Italian, Dutch and Swedish.

Gag at a gnat and swallow a camel, meaning being overly concerned about insignificant matters, while allowing more important ones to escape attention, comes from the *Bible*: Jesus' words to the scribes and Pharisees in *Matthew 23:24*:

"You blind guides, who **strain out a gnat and swallow a camel**!" (*KJV*)

𝒟𝑒𝑒𝑟

The proverbial **deer-in-the-headlights look** is a stunned, blank, lack-of-words facial expression when a person is asked a question that is foreign to his or her understanding or knowledge. The *Chicago Sun-Times*, in late 1999, printed the following:

> "When I ask the tellers about Y2K, I get... **deer-in-the-headlights** stares..."

When a deer is stoically standing on a highway at night and a car approaches, its eyes gaze into the headlights and it seems immobile.

The cliché is American and late 20th century in origin. It came to public recognition during the 1988 presidential campaign of George H.W. Bush. His running mate, Dan Quayle, who of course became the Vice President, after comments made during a debate with Senator Lloyd Bentsen, displayed a blank look which was described by commentators the following day as "like a **deer in the headlights**, frozen in fear."As a result, the statement became a national catch phrase

𝓜𝓪𝓻𝓼𝓾𝓹𝓲𝓪𝓵𝓼

The term **kangaroo court** dates back to at least the mid-19th century, and refers to any mock court which disregards ethical and legal means to bring about what the members feel is swift justice, whether within or outside the legal system. The exact origin is unknown, and so numerous unsubstantiated theories have surfaced as to its coining, including that because kangaroos are native to Australia, it was started there, and 'claim jumping' during the 1849 California Gold Rush. The earliest citation is American, but in spite of a major dictionary placing the first publication of this article in 1853 in Philip Paxton's '*A Stray Yankee in Texas*,' it was actually printed earlier, on July 20, 1850, in *The Literary World*, a New York publication, in 'Drafts at Sight in the Southwest':

"By an unanimous vote, Judge G. — the fattest and funniest of the assembly — was elected to the bench, and the 'Mestang' or '**Kangaroo Court**' regularly organized. Impossible as it would be for one to convey to the reader a correct idea of the ludicrous and supremely ridiculous scene which occurred, I will yet attempt it."

Though here spelled 'mestang,' the alternative term for such a proceeding is mustang court. Notice both are in quotes, indicating a term already coined. Obviously there is an insinuation that this type hastily assembled group is 'jumping to conclusions.'

Play 'possum is an American metaphoric expression used for anything or any person which pretends to be asleep or dead. It is based upon the instinct of opossums which roll over and feign being dead to protect themselves against predators. The date of origin is unclear, but it was in use by 1866 when it was printed in *American Horticulturist*, Volume 25, Orange and Judd, New York in an article about Barn Weevils:

"They are very active in their motions, and, when alarmed, quickly hide themselves, or if touched, **'play possum'** — feigning dead. The female lays her eggs upon the surface of the kernels of grain…"

Happy as a 'possum in a persimmon tree is an American simile which is based on the fact that opossums, nomadic Western marsupials which play dead to avoid human contact, are noted for eating persimmons. Though early examples of the saying in print are illusive, this analogy has been around for many years. An example which would tend to back this up is found in *Focus on Farming*, Volume 4, 1983, page 30:

"After a good meal, and with his favorite pipe going, Granddad would say. 'I'm as **happy as a possum in a persimmon tree.**'"

Small Mammals

Rabbits and hares have long been associated with magic and fantasy. The source of the metaphor **pulling a rabbit out of a hat** is easily understood. This is one of the 'oldest tricks in the book' of the magician. This illusion was popularized by French magician, Herman the Great, in the 19th century, but because so many new illusions have been developed which are much more thrilling, it is no longer a delight to audiences. Actually, it was not nearly as simple a trick as one would think. As a cliché, it has been around since at least the early to mid-20th century and means that someone has success at a task which is totally unexpected. It comes from the idea of getting magical results.

Rabbit hole is used figuratively to typify the path to a disorienting, bizarre and difficult situation; going into the unknown, it is usually stated as 'going down the rabbit hole.' It is taken from Lewis Carroll's *Alice's Adventures in Wonderland*, 1866, page 13:

"...and was just in time to see it pop **down** a large **rabbit-hole** under the hedge. In another moment **down** went Alice after it, never once considering how in the world she was to get out again."

As mad as a March hare derives from the strange behavior of hares during March which is their mating season. It was used as early as the mid-16th century and a version of it was first cited in *The Works of Thomas More, Knyght, Sometyme Lorde*, 1557, printed in Old English, now difficult to render:

"If that mä wer not for malice **as mad** not **as a march hare**, but as a madde dogge y runneth forthe ..."

It was listed verbatim in *The Proverbs, Epigrams and Miscellanies of John Heywood* in 1562:

"95. 'Of the March Hare.' **As mad as a March hare**: where madness compares, [hares? Are not Midsummer hares as mad as March?"

Dust bunnies is a purely figurative term and refers to balls of dust and lint or 'fluff' that accumulate under beds or in corners in a house. A major dictionary lists 1952 as the date of origin. Actual earlier citations are elusive. The term is used in other languages, sometimes as dust mic, as in the German word '*Staubmaus.*' The earliest reference available is from 1980 in *Of Sea and Shore*, Vol. 11-13; page 110:

"Unhappily, baby oil attracts dust, and it is a little embarrassing to show off one's prizes when they are fuzzy and sprinkled with **dust-bunnies**."

Skunk someone is an old metaphor for defeating an opponent overwhelmingly in a game, especially when not allowing the opponent score. It was derived from the fact that when a skunk sprays a person or animal, it completely overwhelms the would-be attacker, preventing any danger to the skunk. The earliest known citation of figurative use is from a story titled "Ingleside Chit-Chat by 'The Squire'" in *The Knickerbocker*, July, 1847, where a priest is making a comparison is between 'The Game of Life' and playing cards. Here is the line from page 14:

"Here he described their appearance, and the emotions which appeared in every face; and then finally ended by saying, that 'while the righteous get High, Low, Jack, and the Game, the sinner gets **skunked** to d...n!'"

The obvious fill in would be 'damnation,' supposedly a word unbecoming to a priest of that day. In the next few years, 'skunked' is used in numerous publications in quotes, indicating recent coining, where here it is cited with no quotation marks, possibly indicating that this is the first figurative use.

We obviously know that the phrase **drunk as a skunk** has nothing to do with the lovable, yet oft avoided furry mammal. It is simply derived from the habit of rhyming our sayings. Though similar expressions in the English language date to the 15th century, 'drunk as a skunk' dates only to the late 1930s. Writers came close in 1938 with citations like this one from *Colliers Illustrated Weekly*, Volume 101:

"**Drunk** and disorderly. Can't you smell it? He was havin' a knock-down- that he was working on an important case, then settled down ... 'You finally sunk to booze and brawlin', eh, you **skunk**?'"

A very early example of a version of the simile is from *American Nabob,* a novel by Holmes Moses Alexander, 1939:

"Half of 'em are **drunk as skunks**."

The next year *Stars on the Sea*, Frances van Wyck Mason, 1940 carried this dead-on line:

"Must have been **drunk as a skunk** not to have recognized him."

The metaphor **eager beaver** describes a very enthusiastic person who does what it takes to be successful at any venture. It is derived from the habits of beavers which appear very industrious and aggressive in building their dams. The earliest form was 'work like a beaver' which dates back to at least June, 1854 when it appeared in quotes, and was stated to be 'significant term,' in *The Journal of Education for Upper Canada*, edited by the Rev, Egerton Ryerson, D.D., in 'The Canadian Beaver' on page 99:

"The *beaver works* always by night, and to '*work like a beaver*' is a significant term for a man who not only *works* earnestly and understandingly—but one who *works* late and early."

While crediting the expression to Canada, a very popular phrase origin book states that 'eager beaver' 'isn't recorded before 1940.' Though actually referring to a beaver, the term appeared in a poem written in 1912, titled, 'In the Mountains,' by M.G. Gowsell, published in the September, 1913 edition of *Râja Yoga Messenger*, in California:

"O're yonder dreams a tiny glade,
A little beauty spot;
A place some **eager beaver** made,
And like as not forgot."

A July 13, 1946 citation of '**Eager Beaver**' is the title Warner Brothers' Looney Tunes cartoon, directed by Chuck Jones and relates to an animated beaver. In less than two years it had developed into a figurative term used as we know it today in America, ands is found in quotes in *The Journal of Health and Physical Education*, January, 1948, in an article titled, 'Technical and Emotional Obstacles which Confront the Physical Educator' by Dr. Lawrence Kubie on page 26:

"As he developed he became an '**eager beaver**.' He did not want to miss out on all athletic triumphs."

Bats, of course, are not birds, but small flying mammals. But there is a fact about these little nocturnal creatures which many may not know. **Blind as a bat** is based on bad information. Bats' eyes are very sensitive, and in daylight they are almost totally unable to see anything. That's why they are called 'blind.' But in the dark, which is when they are up and about, though they have erratic flight patterns, they definitely can see and sense where they are going. In fact, they have a sophisticated built-in sonar system, by which they detect objects around them by sending out ultrasonic sound waves. This simile started in the late 16th century, and has survived the tests of time.

The saying, **bats in the belfry** sounds like an old British movie, or as if it's from a Gothic novel of the 19th century. It is neither. As mentioned above, bats are busy little near-blind winged mammals which fly about in dark places. Belfries are in towers, like church steeples, and were places in which bats dwelt. The earliest record of this is from American writers just after the dawn of the 20th century. For example, this is from an article in *The Newark Daily Advocate*, in Ohio, not New Jersey, in October, 1900:

"To his hundreds of friends and acquaintances in Newark, these purile [sic] and senseless attacks on Hon. John W. Cassingham are akin to the vaporings of the fellow with a large flock of **bats in his belfry**."

The usage here has continued to this day. Someone who is confused and a bit dazzled may be said to have 'bats in the belfry,' or '**gone batty.**'

The old simile **like a bat out of hell** has nothing to do with bats' supposed connection to blood-sucking vampires getting away from their victims to escape capture. The bat is essentially a harmless creature.

This earliest known citation of 'a bat out of hell' appeared in 1915 regarding the speed of a car. It is in *The Southwestern Reporter*, Volume 177, concerning decisions by the Supreme and Appellate Courts:

"They went down onto Main Street and drove out south to Twenty-Third going at so rapid a rate that when they passed Henry McCain and J. H. Martin in another car McCain's attention was attracted to the speed, and he exclaimed: 'It's going **like a bat out of hell!**'"

The article later states that the speed of the car was estimated at 40 to 50 miles an hour—breakneck for 1915. This caused a fatal accident which resulted in a suit (Madding vs. State) which ended up in the Supreme Court of Arkansas on May 17, 1915.

The phrase refers to the uncanny speed of a bat in flight, and the 'out of hell' part is likely to have been added for effect, and probably referred to their abode in dark caves. The Greeks envisioned 'Hades' as underground. Others say it may have come from the German word *höhle* meaning cave.

Though appearing much like a rat, a mole is not actually a rodent. It is a small, beady-eyed, grey soft, furry mammal adapted to a subterranean lifestyle with powerful forearms and paws to burrow in the ground. **Make a mountain out of a molehill** is an oft-used saying which refers to making a 'big deal' out of something insignificant. The first recorded English usage was in 1548. Before that, a mole was known as a 'wand,' later changed to 'want.' A molehill was called a 'want thump.' Still later the name for mole was changed to 'moldewamp,' meaning 'earth thrower.' This was shortened to 'molle.'

The idiom is first found in Nicholas Udall's English translation of *The first tome or volume of the Paraphrase of Erasmus vpon the newe testament*, 1548, recorded below:

> "The Sophistes of Grece coulde through their copiousness **make an Elephant of a flye, and a mountaine of a mollehill**."

It was later recorded in *Foxes Book of Martyrs* in 1570.

Road kill, also spelled 'roadkill' or 'road-kill' is a primarily American colloquialism for an animal killed by a motor vehicle. *Merriam Webster* states 1946 as earliest literal use. Metaphorically, it refers to a person, usually one who falls victim to intense competition. Earliest figurative use is stated by *Etymonline*, the online etymology dictionary, as 1992. This is very close to accurate, and may well be the earliest citation in relation to competition. There is a bit earlier example in print, however, of people as 'road kill' found in the Twin Falls, Idaho newspaper, *The Times News*, Sunday, June 16, 1991, on page C-5, column 5, in 'Turtles help Push Turtles to Extinction':

"...don't become **road kill** yourself,

One more recently coined version is 'political road kill,' which came into usage in the early 21ˢᵗ century.

Not fit for man nor beast is a comical broad ancient saying, which, like road kill, mentions no particular animal.

American musician, composer and lyricist, Billy Strayhorn (1915-1957) is credited for saying, "I'm not fit company for man nor beast." But Strayhorn certainly did not originate the saying, nor did 'fit company' have anything to do with this old adage. The earliest mention of 'man nor beast' is found in the *Torah*, or *Old Testament*, in *Jonah 3:7*:

"Let **neither man nor beast**, herd nor flock, taste any thing: let them not feed, nor drink water:" (*KJV*, 1611)

Authorship of *Jonah* is uncertain, but scholars date the events at circa 760 BC and some who regard it as allegorical date writing of the original text as late as the 4ᵗʰ to 3ʳᵈ century BC. There is evidence that this ancient text inspired our modern saying, as early records refer to tainted water. *The Veterinarian*; a monthly journal of veterinary science, published in London, in the August 6, 1836 issue, contains the following reference on page 4:

"The brook once contained as good water as ever was drunk, and supplied a great many people in the village with water. It is now spoiled, and **not fit for man nor beast**."

History of Mexico Spanish and English Missions of the Methodist Episcopal Church, 1850 – 1910 by Thomas Harwood, Volume I, oddly enough published in 1908, has this citation on page 191:

"The water is clear but impregnated with certain minerals that give the water a bad taste and a very disagreeable odor **not fit for man nor beast.**"

Reptiles

The Americanism **as fine as frog's hair** means someone feels fantastic! We find a citation of it back as far as 1865 in *C. Davis's Diary*:

"I have a better flow of spirits this morning, and, in fact, feel **as fine as frog's hair**, as Potso used to say."

Note, he says, 'Potso *used to say*,' indicating that the phrase had already been around awhile. Obviously, frogs are hairless, and this simile points to the fact that someone feels so fine that there is no feeling quite like it.

The frog does not drink up the pond in which he lives is a proverb which serves as a reminder that the creatures of nature know better than to destroy their environment and know, by nature, how to protect their habitat. Man constantly has been his own worst enemy in the destruction of the earth and its precious resources. This axiom is attributed in a number of modern sources as an Oglala Sioux Tribe Native American saying.

Turtles all the way down is an expression of the infinite regress problem in cosmetology. It is posed by the 'unmoved mover' (something which moves without being moved) paradox. This saying per se goes back to the ancient Hindu myth that a World Turtle supports the earth on its back. This myth further alludes to the belief that this turtle rests on an even larger turtle, which is a part of a column of turtles, each increasing in size, which continues indefinitely.

When this phrase originated is uncertain, but a similar phrase, "rocks all the way down" appeared in print as early as 1838 in a story titled 'Unwritten Philosophy' in the *New York Mirror*, September 15 of that year, on page 91.

> "'The world, marm,' said I, anxious to display my acquired knowledge, 'is not exactly round, but resembles in shape a flattened orange; and it turns on its axis once in twenty-four hours.'
>
> "'Well, I don't know anything about its *axes*,' replied she, 'but I know it don't turn round, for if it did we'd be all tumbled off; and as to its being round, any one can see it's a square piece of ground, standing on a rock!'
>
> "'Standing on a rock! but upon what does that stand?'
>
> "'Why, on another, to be sure!'
>
> "'But what supports the last?'
>
> "'Lud! child, how stupid you are! There's **rocks all the way down**'"

20th century linguist John R. Ross identified American philosopher, William James (1842-1910) with the phrase.

Crocodile tears are a hypocritical show of grief or sadness. The saying derives from the old wives' tale which said that a crocodile wept insincerely if it killed and ate a person.

There are more metaphors having to do with snakes, however, than any other reptile. The imagery of the metaphoric cliché **snake in the grass** goes back to many ancient sources and folklore. The earliest is likely the biblical book of beginnings. In *Genesis 3*, the story is told of how the serpent, or snake, used as a type of the devil, through subtlety, slithered its way into Eve's intellect and convinced her to take a bite of the 'forbidden fruit.'

The origin of the word 'snake' began in the Indo-European root word meaning 'to creep.' This meaning crept down to the Old High German word 'snahhan,' (to crawl), then the Old Norse 'snakr,' and the Old English word, 'snaca.' By Middle English it was already snake.

An ancient Chinese proverb states, "He who is bitten by the snake avoids tall grass."

The snake's craftiness and subtlety coupled with its slithering through the grass to attack its prey has been long used in both literal and figurative senses.

A 'snake in the grass' has come to be an unmistakable image of an untrustworthy, deceitful person.

Crooked as a barrel of snakes is a decidedly Southern American expression first started showing up in print around 1914, when the August issue of *The Practical Druggist*, in an article by W.H. Cousins of Wichita Falls, Texas, titled 'Substitution' contained the following lines:

"If a builder's plans drawn by an architect specified timbers of a given size, and because he could use timbers of much smaller size and have them covered from the sight of the superintendent the builder substituted the smaller timbers and got away with a hundred dollars of another man's money we would all agree that he was **as crooked as a barrel of snakes**."

The comical simile was quickly picked up and was used by a number of other writers in the early 20ᵗʰ century.

The metaphoric phrase **speaks with a forked tongue** means to deliberately say one thing and mean another. It is traditionally associated with the accusations of Native Americans against white men in the days of treaties which were broken by the United States government. This distrust also bled over into the efforts of white missionaries. In *The United States Catholic Magazine*, August, 1846, 'Peré Jean, Or, The Jesuit Missionary, A Catholic Story Founded on Facts,' Chapter IX, tells of the reaction of a Mohawk tribe to the sermon of a missionary:

> "'He **speaks with a forked tongue**,' said Kiohba; 'he is a liar!' 'We are satisfied with our own God,' exclaimed another—'the war-god—Wacondah. The God of the great medicine has made cowards of the Hurons; the God of the Mohawks strengthens the arm of his children in battle.'"

'**Forked tongue**' was used much earlier by Shakespeare in *Henry VI*, Part II, Act I, Scene i, (1591) referring to a snake, the obvious origin:

> "In pain of your Dislike, or pain of Death; Yet notwithstanding such a strange Edict, Were there a Serpent seen with **forked Tongue**, That slyly glided towards your Majesty, It were but necessary you were wak'd…"

The *Bible* pictures the devil as a 'serpent' and a liar. *Psalm 58, verses 3 and 4* speak of lies as being like the poison of a deadly snake.

> "The wicked are estranged from the womb; they go astray as soon as they be born, speaking lies. Their poison is like the poison of a serpent." (*KJV*, 1611).

It is no wonder that throughout history lying and forked tongues have been linked.

The fact that a snake slithers on the ground made **lower than a snake's belly** the perfect simile for low. Then adding '**in a wagon rut**' gets below ground level. It means 'you can't get lower than this' and usually refers to a person's corrupt character, but can also mean that someone feels really poorly.

This metaphor is an Americanism which qualifies as an 'old saying' and the wagon rut indicates about how far back it goes. The earliest known citation in print, however, is from *Everybody's Magazine*, December, 1924:

"I could handle six like you, if they didn't have guns! Men? The only thing about you that's a man's is your pants! You're **lower than a snake's belly**, and that's pretty low!"

The idiom was also used to refer to military planes flying extremely near the ground.

What rock did you crawl out from under? is a figurative, insulting question or any reference to someone 'living under a rock' indicates the speaker's dislike and lack of trust for the other person. Lizards, worms and snakes which normally are found under rocks are not something which most people like to pick up or embrace. The earliest available citation is found in *New York Magazine*, August 1st, 1988, on page 29, in the article, "Last Judgment" by Jeanie Kasindorf:

"At the next break, Mary Koster said to Fink, 'You slime, **what rock did you crawl out from under?**'"

Though now somewhat archaic, the saying, **If it had been a snake it would have bitten you** is often used when a person walks right by an obvious item and does not see it. It can also apply to not seeing something in print, etc. It goes back to at least the late 19th century. It was used by Opie Percival Read in *Emmett Bonlore*, 1891:

"...I didn't see any shirt."

"If it had been a snake it would have bitten you."

"Glad it wasn't a snake."

Cut off the head (of the snake) **and the body dies** is a proverb. When 'the snake' is used, is disputed by those who say that the head can still bite. But where it originated is illusive. The earliest citation with 'a snake,' however, available, seems to come in *Al Qa'ida: Unholy Dogs of War* by Ray Roddy, 2004, chapter 6:

"Al Qa'ida is a snake—**cut off** its head and the **body will die.**"

According to an Associated Press sports story on April 3, 2012, a recording purported to capture former New Orleans Saints defensive coordinator Greg Williams telling players to hurt opponents. He reportedly used the saying **Kill the head and the body will die**, though allegedly in a profane way.

The Watchtower Online Library, in the Czech Republic 2000 Yearbook, published by the Jehovah's Witnesses, carries a story from 1976 in which it is stated that the proverb was used:

"Feb 1, 1976 - They had told Brother Müller when he was in prison: "**Cut off the head, and the body will die.**" They thought that he and other responsible brothers were "the head," but they failed to discern that the real Head of the Christian congregation is the Lord…"

A similar reversed saying is also used, without the snake being mentioned. The quote is from boxer Joe Frazier as found in *Words of Wisdom; More Good Advise* compiled and Edited by William Saphire and Leonard Saphire, 1990, page 363:

'**Kill the body and the head will die**. - Smokin' Joe Frazier'

While we're on this subject, in England, **as mad as a snake** is a saying that goes back to at least January 11, 1868, when it appeared in the London publication, *Punch*, is an article titled "A Fenian with A Chignon" on page 14:

"Why do I take that writer to be a woman? In the first place because she has let the cat out of the bag. In the next, because she writes in the spirit of a woman who is **as mad as a snake**,"

Snake oil is a term which has long been misused. True snake oil originated in China, and is from the Chinese Water Snake. It was used as a cure for rheumatoid arthritis and joint pain. Snake oil also played a role in ancient Egyptian medicine, and was blended with the fats of other animals such as lions, hippopotamuses, crocodiles, etc. It was believed by the masses that it could grow hair on bald men.

Chinese laborers working in America on the trans-continental railroad lines introduced snake oil to Europeans to cure joint pain. There were no regulations in North America in the 19th century regarding drugs, so when charlatans got hold of it, all sorts of fake oils were created. These were hawked by the traveling salesmen who went about the country with their medicine shows selling 'a cure for what ails you' in a bottle to anyone who was gullible enough to fall for their lines.

It was claimed that they often had some who would be paid to testify to the healing properties of their potion. As a result, the term 'snake oil' became used metaphorically for any product with exaggerated marketing but questionable benefits.

Wouldn't hit a lick at a snake is an old contemptuous, hyperbolic saying meaning that a person is so lazy that he or she wouldn't even try to kill a snake if it were about to bite him or her. A 'lick' in this context means a 'blow.' It is an old Southern American slang term. It has likely been in verbal use much longer, but the earliest printed reference available is in Act III of the play *Mule Bone, A Comedy of Negro Life* written in 1930 by Langston Hughes and Zora Hurston, but not produced and preformed until 1964:

"**DAISY** *(Outraged)* Don't you mean to work none?
DAVE Wouldn't hit a lick at a snake."

Section Three

Creepy Crawly Critters

Insects, Bees and Such

To have **ants in one's pants** means to be excessively jittery or anxious. It was coined by the 1930s. Some attribute it to U.S. Army General Hugh S. Johnson who headed the National Recovery Mission in 1933 to 1934. It is certain that he made it popular. The earliest verifiable printed citation is from the **Princeton Alumni Weekly**, May 19, 1939, where is appears in a joking fashion about an alumnus, Jack Plants, and his wife, Loranah St. Clair Plants on their twenty-fifth anniversary:

"It seems only yesterday we were going around the campus singing that old Chaucerian ballad— Rocky Plants' Got **Ants In His Pants**."

It was used by American humorist, H. Allen Smith in his book, *Life in a Putty Knife Factory*:

"She dilates her nostrils a lot, the way Valentino used to do it in the silent movies to indicate that he had **ants in his pants**."

The term antsy, popular in the 1960s likely derived from this saying.

As much fun as ants at a picnic is a sarcastic saying. 'Ants at picnics' has long been a topic of jovial conversation. Obviously, the last thing anyone wants at an outing is ants invading them, which is one of the most likely things to occur. This metaphor was first used by staff writer Kevin Thomas in a *Los Angeles Times* article on June 17, 1988 in regard to the comedy flick, *The Great*

Outdoors, starring John Candy and Dan Aykroyd. Since then it has been used by numerous bloggers, and even best-selling author, David S. Brody in his 2015 novel, *The Isaac Question* in chapter 4, page 95.

"He nodded and sighed. 'You're right. I'm about **as much fun as ants at a picnic.**'"

The rhyming simile, **as snug as a bug in a rug** did not come into being in the 1950s, as some may believe. It first appeared in print in 1769. But the meaning of this curious saying as it was in the 18th century was quite different from today. 'Snug' was then used to mean, 'neat, trim and well-prepared,' specifically as it referred to ships of the day. It had been so defined since at least the latter 16th century.

Before bugs were insects, they were ghosts or spirits. In 1535, the *Cloverdale Bible* uses it in this fashion in *Psalms 91:5*:

"So yt thou shalt not nede to be afrayed for eny bugges by night, ner for arowe that flyeth by daye."

By 1642, however, bug also meant 'beetle' or something like it, as seen in Daniel Rogers' *Naaman the Syrian*.

"God's rare workmanship in the Ant, the poorest bugge that creeps."

As noted in the beginning of this entry, the first known printed reference to 'as snug as a bug in a rug' was in 1769. It is in David Garrick's writings about Shakespeare called *Garrick's vagary, or, England run mad*; with particulars of the Strafford Jubilee.

"If she [a rich widow] has the mopus's [coins or money], I'll have her, **as snug as a bug in a rug.**"

The word 'rug' here, is a Tudor word with the same source as the word 'rag.' But then, rugs were not on the floor, but were thick woolen bed covers, what might today be blankets. So a 'bug in a rug' would have been happy and snug, indeed.

Another strange old simile features a name for a type of bedbug with which most are unfamiliar today. **Crazy as a betsy bug** is a phrase which was once common in the American South; this refers to being uncontrollable, erratic, and irrational. The expression has been around since the late 19th century.

A betsy bug, aka bessie bug, is a member of the Passalidae family of beetles. It is big (about an inch and a half long), black and shiny, and has nasty-looking pincers. It can and will bite people and flies where it wants to.

In 1925, Bernie Babcock used the simile in *Booth and the Spirit of Lincoln: A Story of a Living Dead Man*:

> "A second time this angel came and spoke to Manoah's old woman and a second time he thought her **crazy as a betsy bug**. Then she went down to the water hole to wash — kind of a shady place like under trees."

The date of the origin of the proverb, **Kill one mosquito and a thousand others will come to his funeral**, is unknown, but various forms of it have been around for many years. A similar saying is called a Russian Proverb in an online blog:

> "Do not **kill a single wasp; for then a hundred will come to its funeral**. Russia ..."

In *Roots Web Folk Lore Archives*, the insect is a fly:

> "**Kill one fly and ten flies will come to its funeral**."

A very close example appears in *Laws of the Midge* by Will Copestake:

"Kill one midge and a thousand turn up for its funeral."

Midges are a group of insects which include several types of flies.

Another old expression is **bee line**. In centuries past, most people believed that bees always flew in a straight line to their hives. Therefore, making a 'bee line' for something came to mean going straight for it. An early example is from Charles Dickens, in *All the Year Round, Volume 5*, page 271, 1871, and identifies the phrase as 'American.'

"In America such a line is called '**a bee line**,' and sometimes an 'air line.' Bees, after having laden themselves with honey, have been observed always to fly back to the hive in a direct line, which is not always the case with crows..." (See: As the crow flies.)

A wasp is not technically a bee, but this seems a proper place to include this one. Figuratively, **wasp waist** refers to a woman's very slender waistline. It comes from the fact that a wasp, with its segmented body, has the thinnest waist of any insect. The term was popularized by a style of corset and girdle designed in the 19th century to slenderize a feminine waist, thus exaggerating the hips and bust. The earliest known citation referring to the wasp shape of a woman's figure is found in *The Tattler; or, Lucubrations of Isaac Bickerstaff*, 1764, page 97:

"Our tight-laced grandmothers were nothing to the **wasp**-shaped dames of the court of Catherine de Medicis."

In 1809, 'Helena, the Grecian Beauty' was one of the poems in *The Cypriad in Two Cantos with Other Poems and Translations* by Henry C. Knight published in Boston. The following lines expressed the male view of a wasp waist:

"Her form, it surely was divine,
Compress'd like a **wasp** in the **waist**;
A churn at the bottom so fine,
And other parts all in the taste."

A flea in one's ear is a very old idiom, now meaning an annoying hint or stinging rebuke, has been in use in English since 1430 when it first appeared in the translation of a French devotional work from about 100 years earlier by a Cistercian monk, Guillaume de Deguileville, tilted *The Pilgrimage of the Life of the Manhood*. Mankind, in this case, was referring to the condition of being human. But the French had a bit different interpretation of the phrase, meaning provoking amorous desire, though its intent in the de Degruileville work was spiritual, like the perceived nature of the biblical *Song of Solomon*.

Famed French fabulist and poet, Jean de La Fontaine, used it in the original sense in his 17th century classic narrative, *The Nightingale*:

"A longing girl
With thoughts of sweetheart in her head,
In bed all night will sleepless twirl.
A flea is in her ear, 'tis said."

In ancient times, houses were often infested with fleas and the idea must have been derived from something moving quickly, possibly without forethought, into a person's head. Now, even in French, it has evolved to mean a suspicion in one's head.

Later citations are mixed, but this one, printed in *Corbett's Political Register* on January 4, 1823, in 'Critique of Juan Carlos' on page 27, seems to reflect a change in direction:

"The Ring behaves, indeed, a little more civilly to his wise than the Black man did to his; but he sends her off with a **flea in her**

162

ear, and concludes a long and foolish soliloquy by saying that he will set Valdez and his 'dark troop' to destroy his son!"

Move like the dead lice are falling off of you is an American folk saying going back many years. It means someone is walking far too slowly. In folklore, it is said lice leave the body of a dead person, so this insinuates that a person must be almost dead or he or she could walk faster. It is uncertain where and when this saying originated but likely was coined in the American South in the early-to-mid 20th century.

Maggots are soft bodied, legless larva, particularly of flies, und in decaying matter. It is easy to understand why **gag a maggot** refers to something totally disgusting or revolting. It came into use in the mid-1960s. The earliest citation available is found in *Design with Type* by Carl Dair, 1967:

"'But come on, let's go take a run around the set. Brace yourself, though. I warn you, man, it's terrible — it's ghastly.'

"'Yes, exactly. Ward Four would **gag a maggot**.'"

While we are on the subject of flies, **you can catch more flies with honey than with vinegar** is an very old proverb which means 'kindness is a better way to win friends than anger,' this first appeared in *Piazza universale di proverbi Italiani (A common place of Italian Proverbs and Proverbial Phrases)*, by Giovanni Torriano, F & TW London, 1666. It was recorded in America in 1774 by Benjamin Franklin in *Poor Richard's Almanac*.

If someone in lying in a grassy field, he or she is likely to see grasshoppers hopping about. **Knee-high to a grasshopper** means short, young, or both. The saying was one of many metaphoric analogies originating in the 19th century. One, 'knee-high to a toad,' may have been used as early as 1814. But the first known record in print of this phrase was from the U.S. Magazine, *The Democratic Review*, in 1851.

"You pretend to be my daddies; some of you who are not **knee-high to a grass-hopper.**"

Very closely related to grasshoppers are crickets.

The exclamation **Jiminy Cricket**! originally had nothing to do with these dear little critters, however. It is what is known as a minced oath or euphemism for Jesus Christ. Most people likely believe the saying came about as a result of the jolly conscience of Pinocchio in the 1940 Disney movie; however, this is certainly not the case, but the opposite is true. The talking cricket in Italian author Carlo Collodi's 1883 *The Adventures of Pinocchio*, which first appeared as a serial in 1881 and 1882, was an unnamed minor character, changed to a green grasshopper-like smiling character in Disney's ever-popular cartoon film, was named so because the expression was already in common usage. In 1864, in Charles Reed's *Very Hard Cash*: *A Novel*, page 42, after several statements about the sport of cricket, we find the following:

"'Woman, indeed!' said a treble at the door; 'no more than I am; it's for a young lady. O, **jiminy**'!"

In *Cricket at the Seashore*, 1896, by Elizabeth Westin Timlow, page 315, this snippet uses a 'jiminy' expression close to the word Cricket:

"'Goes down hard enough. Seems to want ilin' or suthin.' Land o' **Jiminy**!' He chanced to turn his head and saw **Cricket** calmly ascending as the pole went higher and higher."

'By Jiminy' was also used around the turn of the century. In *A Bunch of Roses and Other Parlor Plays*, 1903, a play called "His

Lordship," by Mollie Evelyn Moore Davis, has the following on page 65, first published in 1899:

"An' all takin' on over me as if I was--- **Jiminy cricket!**"

Then in 1906 Seymore Seldon Tibbles used the exact expression on page 5 in Act One of another play, *At the Village Post Office: A Musical Play in Two Acts*:

"**Jiminy cricket**, what was that stung me? Must have been a wasp."

The euphemism was well established in movies before Jiminy debuted as a Disney Character, being used in 1937 in the Disney cartoon predecessor of *Pinocchio, Snow White and the Seven Dwarfs*. The saying was spoken by Judy Garland in both *Listen Darling*, 1938, and as Dorothy in the 1939 Classic, *The Wizard of Oz*, when she cried out, "Oh! Oh! **Jiminy Crickets!**" when she was startled by the Wizard's pyrotechnics.

Ward Kimball who worked on *Snow White* actually designed the character.

Often mistakenly attributed to Shakespeare, the well-known proverbial rhyme: "**Oh! What a tangled web we weave when first we practice to deceive**" comes from Sir Walter Scott's *Marmion, Canto VI, Stanza 7*, 1808, which reads in full:

"Yet Clare's sharp questions must I shun
Must separate Constance from the nun
Oh! what a tangled web we weave
When first we practice to deceive!
A Palmer too! No wonder why
I felt rebuked beneath his eye."

There is nothing in a caterpillar that tells you it's going to be a butterfly is a quote from noted American architect, author, environmentalist activist and inventor Richard Buckminster Fuller (1895-1983) which has become proverbial. It is closely related to 'You can't judge a book by its cover' and means that you can't tell a person's potential just by looking at him or her. We must allow each person to change with time, and become the individual that he or she is destined to become.

And speaking of butterflies, someone with **butterflies in his or her stomach** feels nervous, queasy and jittery. The person may be scared or excited by circumstances. Anxiety can cause a disruption of the body's enzymes. It is claimed that once a clever writer used the metaphor and it caught on. Some have used it to relate to the special emotion of new love. Many folks believe that they are only psychological, but an article in *Science News* by Joanne Silberner back on February 22, 1986 entitled '*Stomach Butterflies Scramble EGGs*' (erratic electrogastrograms) states, "**Butterflies in your stomach** aren't all in your head."

A snail's pace is an idiom, meaning moving ridiculously slow and dates back to Middle English in the early 15th century according to leading etymologists. Snails are said to be the epitome of slow. Sometimes this is used sarcastically to describe some process that is seen as inefficient. The lightening-fast electronic world of email today has made the future of the Postal Service seem dismal. Traditional mail is now often referred to as 'snail mail.'

We've all heard it said that doing something would **open up a can of worms**. This metaphor is based on worms which were sold in cans for fish bait in the U.S. in the 1950s. Once they were opened, it was very hard to get the can shut so that the worms could not escape. Opening or getting into a can of worms became a figurative expression for bringing to light a matter which caused more problems than it did good and was not easily resolved. In spite of claims by other sources that the earliest citation is from 1955, *The Bulletin for Atomic Scientists*, January, 1951, page 6, contains the following figurative connotation in "An address (by

Robert J. Oppenheimer) delivered to the Awards Banquet of the Science Talent Institute in Washington, D.C., March 6, 1950":

"Perhaps nowhere has the impact of science more clearly altered the specific terms of a great political issue in the effects of political development on warfare. This is **a can of worms** with which I have myself unhappily been engaged for some years. It would not be honest to say— though it would not be foolish to hope— that the very terror of modem weapons would in itself put an end to war…"

Pesky Rodents

Mice and rats are universally despised, except for the domesticated ones which have won the hearts of their keepers. The gnomic idiom **when the cat's away the mice will play** fits into two sections, but was saved purposely for this group. It means that when the person in authority is absent, the subordinates are apt to take advantage of their freedom by breaking rules because some workers lack self-discipline. Though earlier versions existed in both Latin, *Dum felis dormit, mus gaudet et exsi litantro* (When the cat falls asleep, the mouse rejoices and leaps from the hole) and early 14th century French, *Ou chat na rat regne* (Where there is no cat, the rat is king), the first English usage was in Middle English, circa 1470 in **Harley MS 3362**, as listed in **Retrospective Review**, 1854:

"The mows lordchypythe [rules] ther a cat ys nawt"

A version of it was then used by Shakespeare in **Henry V**, I, ii, 1599:

"To her unguarded nest the weasel Scot Comes sneaking, and so sucks her princely eggs, **Playing the mouse in absence of the cat.**"

Among other citations, it was listed as we now know it in John Ray's **A Hand-book of English Proverbs**, 1670:

"**When the cat is away, the mice play.**"

Speaking of mice metaphors involving people, **The best laid plans of mice and men often go awry** is another very familiar one. Many likely thought that this was coined by John Steinbeck in his classic novel, later made into an epic motion picture, *Of Mice and Men*. However, it was Robert Burns who first penned these immortal words (or a close, rather Scottish, version) in his narrative poem, *To a Mouse*.

The section goes like this:

"But Mousie, thou are no thy-lane,
In proving foresight may be vain:
The best laid schemes o' Mice an' Men,
Gang aft agley,
An' Lea'e us nought but grief an' pain,
For promised joy."

The phrase relates to the fact that no matter how much planning someone does, 'a monkey wrench' can always be thrown into the equation foiling them.

The idea of being **quiet as a mouse** dates back to the 1500s. A mouse was viewed as the quintessential example of a quiet creature. The thought was expressed in 1562 **in *Proverbs, Essays and Miscellanies of John Heywood*** in a poem:

"A **Quiet** Neighbour. ... I never heard thy fire once spark; I never heard thy dog once bark; I never heard once in thy house So much as one peep of one **mouse**; I never heard thy cat once mew — These praises are not small nor few."

Then we find the exact simile in 1750 in Charles Leslie's translation of alchemist Philalethes' 17th century Latin writings, which he deemed 'pernicious,' *A View of the Times, Their Principles and Practices: Volume I*, which he called *The Rehersal*, page 78:

"And if we had been let alone, we should have been as **quiet as a mouse** in a cheese."

To **smell a rat** means something is suspicious; like the Shakespearean quote from Hamlet, "Something is rotten in the state of Denmark." This goes back centuries, to the time when rats were common pests and carried diseases. Wealthy people would obtain dogs, which had a keen sense of smell, to sniff out the rats and get rid of them. When one of these dogs would perk up his ears and begin sniffing around, it was believed that he 'smelled a rat.'

This came, as many sayings regarding animals have, to be personified.

Cunning as a dunny rat is Aussie slang for very shrewd and conniving. A 'dunny' was originally, since the 1930s, an outside toilet, but now can be used for any toilet. Sometimes the saying is shortened to merely 'dunny rat' when referring to an individual, as in Southerly, *The Magazine of the Australian English Association*, Sydney, Volume 53, 1993, page 74:

"Is that what you called me over to see, you stinking **dunny rat**?"

Section Four

Birds of a Feather

𝓑𝓮𝓵𝓸𝓿𝓮𝓭 𝓑𝓲𝓻𝓭𝓼

Though some of our '**fine feathered friends**' are covered in the first section of Home and Farm Fowl, we will now turn our attention to those most likely found only in the wild.

A lot of people seem to think the expression **fine feathered friends** originated with the 1942 one-reel animated Tom and Jerry cartoon produced by Hannah and Barbera released by Metro Goldwyn Mayer with this title. Then others felt that it started just a bit further back with the 1937 big-band hit by Glen Miller, *My Fine Feathered Friend*. In actuality, it's a lot older than that. A novel published in 1751 by British author Robert Paltock titled *The Life and Adventures of Peter Wilkins* first held this strange phrase. In it Wilkins stumbled into an underground society of flying people to whom he refers as his "**fine-feathered friends**," and married one of them named Youwarkee. The saying through the 20th century came to be used jokingly of old friends or people who are nice-looking and well-dressed, in an allusion to colorful birds.

Birds of a feather flock together, meaning that persons of similar interests are likely to find each other and keep company, has been around at least since the mid-16th century. William Turner used a form of it in his 1545 'papist satire' (writing against the Roman Catholic religion) *The Rescuing of Romish Fox*.

"**Byrdes of an kynde** and coulor **flok** and flye always together."

A bird in the hand is worth two in the bush is a common ancient proverb, meaning a small advantage or known asset is more valuable to a chance at a larger profit. This particular version goes back to medieval days when falcons were commonly used as birds of prey. It meant that the falcon was very valuable to its owner and certainly worth more than two birds not yet obtained (in the bush).

How far back this was actually in use is debated. A similar proverb is found in Solomon's biblical book of *Ecclesiastes* chapter *9*, verse *4,* written circa 938 BC. '**A living dog is better than a dead lion.**' This was first in English in *Wycliff's Bible* in 1382.

The 7th century Aramaic *Story of Ahikar* has text that modern translations render as "**Better is a sparrow held tight in the hand than a thousand birds flying about in the air.**"

The earliest form of this proverbial saying is first found in English in John Capgrave's *The Life of St Katharine of Alexandria*, 1450:

"**It is more sekyr [certain] a byrd in your fest, Than to haue three in the sky a-boue.**"

An even closer version is quoted in a book of proverbs by John Heywood in 1546 titled *A dialogue conteinying the number in effect of all the prouerbes in the Englishe tongue*. This version was printed as: '**Better one byrde in the hande than ten in the wood.**'

Then the Scottish version was recorded in John Ray's *A Hand-Book of Proverbs*. 1670, page 226:

"**Ae bird i' the hand is worth ten fleeing.**"

Other European countries have also versions of this saying.

The Bird in Hand was used as a common name for English pubs in the Middle Ages, and several still exist today. A hamlet in Pennsylvania founded in 1734 was given that name.

The early bird gets (or **catches**) **the worm** is a proverb which means that when someone puts in the proper effort and prepares well, he or she will reap rich rewards. Though it may be older, it was first recorded by, and came down to us from, John Ray in *A Compleat Collection of English Proverbs*, 1678:

"**The early bird catcheth the worm.**"

The simile **wise as an owl** is based purely on myth, since owls are not really wise, and have a smaller brain than most other birds. It comes from Greek mythology, and likely was inspired by the serious look and bright, wide-awake eyes of the species. An owl cannot even move its eyes, but obtains its peripheral vision form turning its head from side to side. In *Fables* by John Gay, 1728, on page 124 we read these poetical lines in Fable XXII, 'The Two Owls and the Sparrow:'

"I grant you were at Athens grac'd,
And on Minerva's helm were placed,
But ev'ry bird that wings the sky,
Except an *owl*, can tell you why.
From hence they taught their schools to know
How false we judge by outward show,
That we should never looks esteem,
Since fools as *wise* as you might seem."

An old nursery rhyme, first published in *Punch* on April 10, 1875 is titled, '**A Wise Old Owl**:'

"There was an **owl** liv'd in an oak
The more he heard, the less he spoke
The less he spoke, the more he heard.
O, if men were all like that **wise** bird"

Eagles represent the highest levels of bird life. They are portrayed in metaphors as having the sharpest vision, being the most determined and even the bearers of our paychecks.

Eagle-eyed refers to a person's ability to observe closely or pay great attention to detail. The earliest reference in print to this expression is in *Rofallnde Eupheus golden legacie: Memoir of Thomas Lodge* by Edmond W. Gosse, 1590, page 11:

> "Climbe not my fonnes, afpiring pride is a vapour that afcendeth hie, but soone turneth to a fokmaoke: those which ftare at the Starres, stumble vppon stones; and fuch as gaze at the Sunne (vnlesse they bee **Eagle eyed**) fall blinde."

Note here the Early Modern English spellings; v's used for u's and f's for s's in numerous cases. Also, at this stage, the present meaning did not seem to have yet evolved.

By 1619, it appears that the intent of the expression was developing to be observant. The following is from *A Bride-bush, Or, A Direction for Married Persons*, by William Whately, page 166:

> "To be fomewhat purblind in feeing faults, is leffe dangerous, than to be **eagle-eyed**. In such nearenesse and inwardnesse of conuersation, it is impossible, but that diuers wants shall offer themfelues to bee feene."

I have a large plaque on my office wall with a striking bronze eagle. Under it is a metal plate on which is engraved a congratulatory etching headed by the words, **Eagles dare to win**. I am very proud of this plaque, because it was presented to me in recognition for a highly successful year in my career. This catch phrase has been used since the MGM 1968 World War II film, *Where Eagles Dare*, starring Clint Eastwood and Richard Burton brought the 'eagles dare' theme to front and center.

Eagles are a symbol of bravery, and the National bird of America. *Inc. Volume 2* in 1980 contained the following:

"Eagles Dare to Win ... One of these 'psychological triggers' is the Eagle."

Payday for most working class people is traditionally Friday. As a result, the phrase **the eagle flies on Friday** has come to be used as a cliché and songs have included it since 1947 when T Bone Walker's *Call it Stormy Monday* was released containing the following bluesy lyric:

"Yes **the eagle flies on Friday**, and Saturday I go out to play
Eagle flies on Friday, and Saturday I go out to play
Sunday I go to church, then I kneel down and pray"

Another bird viewed positively is the lark. **As happy as a lark** was in use as a simile in English as early as the late 18th and early 19th centuries.

As happy as a lark is derived from the cheerful song of this beautiful and common songbird. One example is from the New York publication, *Puck, Volume 10*, Issue 103, 1882:

"On, on we went, and I began to feel **as happy as a lark**, when what do you suppose happened?"

Birds have long been the bearers of messages, particularly carrier pigeons. **A little bird told me** is a saying which has its basis in the *Bible*. Solomon wrote in *Ecclesiastes 10:20* that we should not curse the king, or the rich, even in private, or 'a bird of the air' may report what we say. Being one of the most powerful kings of the day he had the authority to squelch such gossip aimed his way.

Also seen is a pleasing light are cardinals. **A cardinal is a visitor from heaven**, also stated as **Cardinals appear when angels are near**, is a modern proverbial saying used to indicate that deceased loved ones appear in the image of cardinals. It is derived from an old Native American tradition which holds the spiritual belief that spirits, or souls, inhabit the universe. The belief that all birds and other animals, known as power or medicine animals, are messengers from the Great Spirit has long been an element of shamanism. Cardinal medicine symbolizes relationships, courtship and monogamy in Native American lore. This has carried over into Catholic teachings, as red is said to represent the blood of Christ, Beginning in 2014, this idea was popularized on social media sites.

Free as a bird means that one has no obligations to others, and is at liberty to do anything he or she wishes. A major online dictionary states coining at 1700, however, earliest verifiable citations come from the early 1800s, with the first being *Wild Flowers, Or, Pastoral and Local Poetry* by Robert Bloomfield, in 'The Broken Crutch' on page 54:

"A novice quite:—he past his hours away,
Free as a bird and buxom as a day."

And don't forget, the term **love birds** is applied to those who are lovers. A lovebird is one of nine species of the genus Agapornis, taken from the Greek words *agape* 'love' and *ornis* 'bird.' They are small, colorful parrots which are very affectionate, native to tropical climates. The earliest known verifiable citation of what *seems to be* humans being called love birds is in Charles Dickens' serialized novel, *Bleak House*, 1852-1853:

"Mr. Guppy, going to the window tumbles into a pair of **love-birds**, to whom he says in his confusion, 'I beg your pardon, I am sure.'"

Dreaded Birds

Symbolic signs and superstitions are widely recognized in every culture. A popular belief is that seeing a blackbird fly nearby indicates impending death.

Speaking of death, **as dead as the dodo** has reference to someone who, or something which, for all practical purposes, is as dead as the long extinct bird. The dodo was native to Mauritius, a volcanic island nation in the Indian Ocean, and was last seen alive by Dutch explorers in 1662 and thought to have died out by 1690.

In November, 1890 *The Cornhill Magazine* first printed an article titled 'Big Birds' which used this analogy, later reprinted in *Littell's Living Age*, apparently triggering the advent of the simile.

"The cats and pigs helped in the slaughter by eating the defenceless eggs and callow young; and half a century after the Dutchman came **the dodo** was as **dead** as Julius Caesar."

Then, on December 6, 1899, the actual simile was cited in an article titled 'Small Talk of the Week' in *The Sketch, a Journal of Art and Actuality*:

"Whether such an apparently Utopian association will ever exist depends upon the revival, under strong leadership, of an esprit de corps among playwrights which at the present time is **as dead as the dodo**."

Crows are large black birds which, like starlings and blackbirds, pose a threat to corn crops. **As the crow flies** is a universal phrase coined in the U.K. and has been long used in Scotland to denote the shortest route, likely because of the presence of many crows there. The choice of a crow, other than for this reason, seems inappropriate, since their flight patterns are not notable for their straightness, and they frequently fly in long arcs in search of food.

The first known printed citation is from the *London Review of English and Foreign Literature* by W. Kenrick, 1767.

"The Spaniard, if on foot, always travels **as the crow flies**, which the openness and dryness of the country permits; neither rivers nor the steepest mountains stop his course, he swims over the one and scales the other."

Crow's feet, also known as 'laugh lines' or 'character lines,' refers to the inevitable tiny wrinkles on the outside of a person's eyes which begin form early in adulthood, and often become more pronounced with the aging process. According to *Random House Dictionary*, this term originated in this context somewhere between 1350 and 1400. The earliest known citation is in Chaucer's epic poem, *Troilus and Criseyde* (circa 1385). Having just been told by Xander that the wrinkles in the corners of his eyes "kinda looked like bird tracks," Buffy replied:

"'What?' Eyes widening in horror, Buffy immediately reached up to touch the area in question. '**Crow's feet**? I've got crow's feet? I'm too young to have **crow's feet**!'"

Eating crow, as an idiom, originated in the U.S. in the mid-19th century. It symbolizes the humility of someone who was overly sure about something, and found out that he or she was wrong.

The exact origin is obscure, but it may have begun with an American story published by that exact name in San Francisco's *Daily Evening Picayune* on 3 December 1851 about a simple farmer in Lake Mahopack, New York. Other tales with similar titles, however, were printed around that time, even a bit sooner.

The crow is one of the birds listed in the *Bible* in *Leviticus 11* which was considered unfit to eat, or 'unclean' under Hebrew law. The crow is in the scavenger class with the likes of the raven, the vulture and the buzzard. A Currier and Ives painting by Thomas Worth in 1883 is called "**Eating Crow** on a Wager."

These undesirable fowl are the most likely for farmers to be throwing stones at. Even killing one bird by throwing a stone, however, would likely be rare. **Kill two birds with one stone** is a humorous metaphor. The intent, of course, is taking care of two needs with a single effort.

Though there were similar phrases used in English and French literature in the 16th century, the earliest known printed reference to this idiom, as we use it today, was by Thomas Hobbes in *A Work on Liberty* in 1656.

"T. H. thinks to **kill two birds with one stone**, and satisfy two arguments with one answer."

For the birds is a figure of speech applied to something which is thought to be trivial or worthless, not worthy of one's attention. There is more than one theory as to how it came to mean this. The earliest citations of something being for the birds are in Old Testament biblical passages. *Isaiah 8*, which, after stating that unproductive shoots will be cut off before the harvest of fruit, in verse *6* (*KJV*, 1611) says:

"They will all be left for the birds of the hills and the wild animals…"

Jeremiah 16:4 says that the corpses of those killed in war "will be food **for the birds** and the wild animals…"

Both verses are speaking of something which is undesirable being 'for the birds.'

Another source states that before the advent of automobiles in New York City, the manure dropped by horses pulling wagons caused a lot of stink. The horses were served oats, so it was suggested that the undigested oats be used to feed a large population of English sparrows. According to this source, saying something was 'for the birds' was saying it was 'horse manure.'

Another popular source says that it originated near the end of World War II as army slang. An article in October, 1944, in *The Lowell Sun*, Lowell, Massachusetts, quotes Sergeant Buck Erickson, of Camp Ellis, Illinois as saying:

"Don't take too seriously this belief that we have football at Camp Ellis solely for the entertainment of the personnel – that's strictly **for the birds**. The army is a winner… the army likes to win – that's the most fortunate thing in the world for America."

But this is a bit late, as there is a plain reference to the saying in *Jobber Skald*, a novel by British author, John Cowper Powys, 1935, on page 119:

"'I told him it was a piece of silliness,' she said in her heart as she snatched those furtive glances of the Mangel Road….with a fling of her arm. 'That's **for the birds**!' she said aloud. But the phrase carried no mental or physical image with it, either of birds or of anything else. All that it carried with it was a passionate desire to tell Magnus right out that she could not possibly marry him."

The slang metaphoric expression, **bird-brained**, means lacking in seriousness or maturity; foolish or scatterbrained. The earliest known citation of this expression is found in *The Century*

Illustrated Magazine, August, 1910 in a story titled 'Mrs. Northmere's Treasure' by Gertrude Hall:

"She was burdened with overstanding debts of her son's, with the support of a **bird-brained**, extravagant, in dirigible daughter-in-law, with doctors and luxuries and changes of air to furnish for Innesley."

A final off-beat metaphor using the word bird is **jailbird.** This term refers to a person who has been incarcerated on more than one occasion. The word jail was originally spelled 'goal;' thus, the word was first, 'goal bird.' The earliest reference in print comes from ***The Scotch Rogue, or Life and Actions of Donald MacDonald***, page 66, 1706:

"But as luck wou'd have it, I quickly after met with my **Goal-Bird**-Companions; who had promis'd me such mighty things in Prison; he Was over-joy'd to see me, and especially at such a time when he told me he cou'd serve me…"

Unlike their eagle cousins, hawks are more dreaded predators. But like eagles, they are known to have acute vision. **Watch someone like a hawk** means very closely and carefully. This can refer to making certain that they do not do something they are not supposed to do, or to keep them under surveillance so they won't escape. Many citations showed up in print in the early 20th century. An interesting example is in ***Happy Valley***, by popular American novelist, John Fox, Jr. 1917, on page 116:

"If you don't **watch him like a hawk** while I'm gone I reckon James Henry'll larn them younguns o' yours all the devilment in the world."

Section Five

Fish & Other Water Creatures

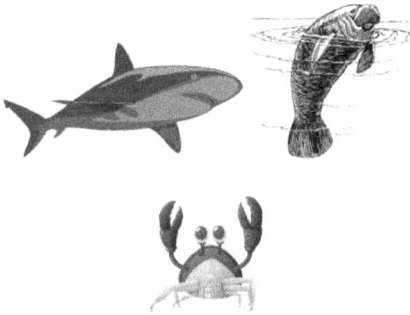

Strictly Fishes

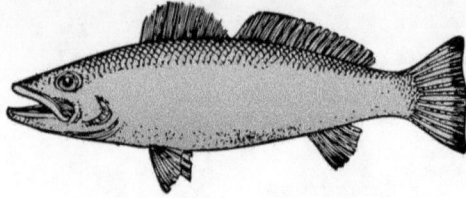

A **big fish in a small pond** is someone with great abilities and much pull in a small company or geographical area. A reverse to this would be a **small fish in a big pond**.

The phrase is from the U.S. and the earliest reference seems to be in *The Galveston Daily News*, in Texas, in June 1881, and apply to local interests:

"They are **big fish in a small pond**."

In 1919, both phrases were used in the *Engineering and Mining Journal*, Volume 107, published by the American Institute of Mining Engineers:

"I would rather be a **big fish in a small pond** than a **small fish in a big pond**."

Since the 1980s the expression has gained much popularity and has been used by writers in books of almost every genre.

Humans have been catching fish as a food source since the dawn of time. **Give a man a fish and you'll feed him for a day; teach a man how to fish and you'll feed him for a lifetime** is such an old proverb that its origin has faded into the fogs of history. At times it been credited to 'a Native American saying,' 12th century Rabbi Moshe ben Maimon, and even the *Bible*! But it is most often attributed to ancient Chinese philosopher, Lao Tse (circa 599 AD).

No verifiable evidence has been found for any of this. The earliest citation in print of a form of it in English, however, is from the 1885 novel, *Mrs. Dymond*, by British author Anne Isabella Thackeray Ritchie (the daughter of William Makepiece Thackery):

"'I don't suppose even Caron could tell you the difference between material and spiritual,' said Max, shrugging his shoulders. 'He certainly doesn't practise his precepts, but I suppose *the Patron* meant that **if you give a man a fish he is hungry again in an hour. If you teach him to catch a fish you do him a good turn**. But these very elementary principles are apt to clash with the leisure of the cultivated classes. Will Mr. Bagginal now produce his ticket—the result of favour and the unjust sub-division of spiritual environments?' said Du Parc, with a smile."

Most sport fishing is done with a fishing pole, which has a hook and sinker at the end of the line. **Hook, line and sinker** is a common idiom; usually 'swallowed (something) hook, line and sinker,' but at other times 'fell for (something) hook, line and sinker' It means to believe something at once without considering its source or testing its authenticity. It is often used to describe how someone thought to be gullible reacts to stories told them by others.

Originating in the United States in the mid-19th century, it is an extension of an earlier English saying, 'to swallow a gudgeon.' A gudgeon is a tiny fish used for bait. The idea implies that the gullible person is like a starved fish which swallows not only the bait, but the entire hook, line and sinker.

Either fish or cut bait is one of several either/or sarcastic ultimatums, such as 'put up or shut up.' It most commonly means to do something worthwhile or get out of the way so someone else can do the job.

The phrase originated in the U.S. in the mid-19th century. Cut bait is when a small fish is cut up to use for bait to catch larger ones. The Utica, New York publication, *The Opal: A Monthly Periodical of the State Lunatic Asylum*, printed this in 1852:

"But delicacy is attacked with Epilepsy in depicting so faithfully the results of sane life; the truth needs no commentary; farther, the moral turpitude of such customs, among those who profess so loud, and long, their fortunate position among folks; and hence, their infallibility bids him who indulges his time to pass in their narration, to **fish or cut bait**."

Not exactly the best reference to judge the phrase. However, the very next year the expression made a larger splash when it appeared in a publicized land dispute between Caleb Cushing, then Attorney General for the U.S., and William Hungerford. The judge on the case was Levi Hubble, and Hungerford was so unhappy with his decision that he tried to have Hubble impeached. His response hit the national news. This is from the official record of impeachment proceedings in Wisconsin in June, 1853:

"Judge Cushing has commenced a suit in the United States Court. Judge Cushing must **either fish or cut bait**."

But the expression was so foreign to the attorneys that they didn't know what to say. One of many evidences of this was in the *Milwaukee Daily Sentinel* in August:

"There was some discussion amongst counsel, without any conclusion, as to the meaning of this phrase."

But by 1856, the figurative usage seemed to have caught on and was appearing in various other American publications. A similar phrase is 'Lead, follow or get out of the way.'

Like shooting fish in a barrel, a metaphor meaning that something is ridiculously easy, is derived from the fact that fish used to be packed in barrels. When someone shoots, particularly a shotgun, into a school of fish, many will die from the mere shock of the blast. This practice is, of course, illegal in many locales, but it has been done by unscrupulous persons many times, and is undoubtedly the simplest way to kill the most fish at once. The earliest known citation is from 1949 in *American Business, Volume 19*:

"**LIKE SHOOTING FISH IN A BARREL** It's a cinch to get urgently needed facts and figures when all you have to do is call STATISTICAL."

Then the term took off in 1958 when UCLA folklore and music teacher Donald K. Wilgus published *Shooting Fish in a Barrel: the Child Ballad in America*.

Then, Sonny Liston talked of a fight with Joe Frazier, claiming "it'd be **like shooting fish in a barrel**." (November 18, 1958: Auditorium, Miami Beach, Florida)

In the October 20th issue of *Billboard* that same year, the following appeared on page 42:

"Bentley said that if the weather is good, that date PHONEMEN ADDING 4 MORE PHONES **Like shooting fish in a barrel**."

Like a fish out of water refers to someone in a position for which he or she is totally unsuited. It is very old, and a form of it was used by Chaucer in *The Canterbury Tales: Prologue*, 1386:

"...a monk, when he is cloisterless;
Is **like to a fish that is waterless**."

The earliest known reference to the current idiom is in *Pilgrimage*, by Samuel Purchas, 1613:

"The Arabians out of the desarts are as **Fishes out of the Water.**"

Speaking of fish out of water, **green around the gills** is a hyperbolic statement sometimes made jestingly and good-naturedly. It is usually said to someone who appears sick because of a reaction to something eaten or done, and that he or she may regurgitate. Gills are the respiratory organs of aquatic animals and fish, which enable them to breathe underwater. It has been around since at least 1906 when it appeared in *The Motorboat*, a bi-monthly New York magazine, in the July 10 edition:

"The effect was so very marine that, when Mrs. Willie Reefer Jibb and Mrs. Shiver R. Timbers, of Gowanus, saw the costume they were both seized with a violent attack of nausea and **turned green around the gills.**"

One of the oldest and most common ways to prepare fish to eat is by frying them. Versions of the old saying, **have bigger** or **other fish to fry**, are popular in several languages including French, German and Spanish. It means that there are more pressing matters at hand. It is claimed by another popular cliché origin book that it was coined in *Memoirs* the diary of John Evelyn, written in the early 1700s, first published until 1818.

However, it appeared much earlier, in *The Works of Francis Rabelias* published by the Navarre Society in London in 1653:

"Do'st thou think, continu'd my Lord, thou 'rt in the Wilderness of your foolish University, wrangling and bawling among the idle, wandring Searchers and Hunters after Truth? By Gold, we **have here other Fish to fry**, we go another-gat's way to work, that we do..."

Fish and company stink after three days is a well-used proverb which may have been gleaned from 'the wisdom of the ages,' but was passed down to us by Ben Franklin as '**fish and visitors stink after three days**' and was included in *Poor Richard's Almanac*.

A fish always rots from the head down is a popular proverb, especially in the U.K, meaning that the problems in an organization or a country almost certainly can be traced to its leadership. It is very old, and forms of it are used in many European cultures; several countries claim it, so pinpointing its true origin is difficult. According to Professor Wolfgang Mieder, chairman of the department of German and Russian at the University of Vermont, and the author of *The Politics of Proverbs, From Traditional Wisdom to Proverbial Stereotypes*, 1997, the earliest citation of this saying was in a treatise titled *An Account of the Voyage to New England*, 1674. It could be even older, as one claim is that it was used in a Greek text by Erasmus who died in 1546, but that text is not available for verification. The Persian poet Rumi, who died in 1273, actually gave us the principle when he included this line in his *Third Book of Poetry*:

"**Fish begins to stink at the head, not the tail.**"

Of course this English translation was done centuries later.

If wishes were fishes, we'd all have a fry is an interesting proverb to trace. The following is found in *Harper's Magazine* in September, 1874, in a story titled *In the Abess's Parlor* by Frank Lee Benedict:

"Jem once more quavered out, '**If fishes were wishes—**"

This is derived from an age-old rhyme appearing in *The Children's Pew* by J. Reid Howatt, 1893, where it was referred to as an 'old rhyme':

"**If wishes were fishes,
We'd all have some fried**;
If wishes were horses,
Beggars would ride."

Another version is found in the London literary publication *Pick-Me-Up*, 27 August 1892, in a poem titled, *"If Wishes Were Aught,"* of which this is one verse:

"If wishes were horses, Beggars would ride;
If wishes were fishes,
We'd swim with the tide;
If wishes were aught but a fanciful thought,
Love only would abide."

This is a variation of an earlier Scottish proverb from James Kelly's *A Complete Collection of Scottish Proverbs*, 1721, which says "If wishes were horses, beggars would ride."

All rhymes and proverbs regarding wishes remind us that they are elusive.

Everyone is a genius, but if you judge a fish by its ability to climb a tree, it will spend its whole life thinking it is stupid is a quote from Albert Einstein (1879 –1955). It is a thought-provoking reminder to not judge anyone by your personal abilities or agenda. All of us have different talents and those are the criteria by which others view us.

The most dreaded of all fish is likely the shark. Therefore this term, when used metaphorically, has often taken unpleasant turns. An unscrupulous attorney is called a shark. Someone who charges excessive interest rates to loan money to someone who is desperate and seemingly has no other choice to obtain the money is dubbed a **loan shark**. Usually these people are involved with an organized crime syndicate. The term is American in origin and, though the practice began earlier, and the word 'shark,' was used as early as 1569 in a handbill distributed in London:

"There is no proper name for it that I knowe, but that sertayne men of Captayne Haukinses doth call it a '**sharke**.'"

The word was defined as "a dishonest person who preys on others" or "an artful swindler" as early as 1594 according to *Etymonline*, the online etymology dictionary, which states that 'loan shark' was first attested in 1905. It is most commonly thought to have derived from the marine shark which viciously attacks people. The earliest source available, however, is from *The Campaign Against the Loan Shark* by Arthur H. Hamm, published by the Department of Remedial Loans, Russell Sage Foundation in New York in 1912, and *The Implet*, Volume 1, January to June, published by Imp Films Company, also in New York, in 1912 by Thomas Bedding, which contains numerous citations.

Red herring is a metaphor, often used in crime mysteries, which refers to something used to distract one from discovering the truth. Perhaps a supposed clue planted to make someone other than the perpetrator appear to be guilty. It derives from the fact that when herrings are smoked, they turn red and give off a strong odor. In the past, smoked herrings have been used to teach hunting dogs to follow a trail. They were taken across the path of the animal being followed to distract the hounds; then taught to overcome the distraction and continue in pursuit of the prey. The earliest known reference in print to the literal use is from *Roberts' Semi Monthly Magazine,* April 1, 1841, in 'The Poacher,' a novel being printed as a serial, by 'Captain Marryat,' in Chapter XIV:

"'To trail! I think they're fast enough upon our *trail* already; but if you want to help them, a **red herring**'s the thing.'"

The first available figurative use is found in *The Public,* Saturday June 30, 1903:

"Maybe he intended vaguely to get pensioned out of land values anyhow, and Mr. Chamberlain has sprung the imperial protection scheme to throw him off the landlord scent. However that may be, the scent is there, and if the British workingman once gets on the trail of it no **red herring** is likely to divert him."

Other Sea Creatures

Like a lobster pot is a British simile. Lobster pots are enticing traps for catching lobsters, and have been in use since at least 1764. They were traditionally made of wood, but now are plastic, and are known for being secure in holding their catch. Lobsters are lured in through a tunnel or 'chamber' of netting into the parlor which holds the bait. In British English, this saying has come to refer to something you can crawl into but cannot get out of or something you have agreed to, only to find that there isn't a cancellation clause. A modern example in print is from *Eternal Fragments* by Francis Castro, 2010, page 29:

"Irony is **like a lobster pot**. It's a trap only for the lobster's insipience."

Slick as an eel is an American simile for 'so slippery it is difficult to hold' has been in usage since at least the 1830s. The earliest known example in print is from *Philadelphia Scrapbook and Gallery of Comicalities*, Saturday, 17 May 1834:

"Well, as I could git no satisfaction from the Captain, I took a good pull of switchel and laid down on a hen coop to look out for squalls, when I didn't soon see one, leaning towards us, that in an hour made the *beauty* hoe it off through the water jist as **slick as an eel** — though the poor thing lost the bonnet from her gib in the confusion."

ALPHABETICAL INDEX

A

All bark and no bite	12
All hat and no cattle	87
Ants in one's pants	158
As brave as a lion	120
As fine as frog's hair	149
As happy as a lark	176
As healthy as a horse	53
As mad as a March hare	141
As much fun as ants at a picnic	158
As nervous as a cat on a hot tin roof	28
As nervous as a long-tailed cat in a room full of rocking chairs	29
As rare as hen's teeth	102
As sick as a parrot	115
As snug as a bug in a rug	159
As the crow flies	179
As useless as tits on a boar hog	48

B

Barking orders   12

Barking up the wrong tree   12

Bats in the belfry   145

Be a canary in a coal mine   116

Beat a hen a-pecking / a rootin'   103

Beating a dead horse   67

Bee line   161

Beggar on horseback   61

The best laid plans of mice and men often go awry   169

Big fish in a small pond   184

Bird-brained   182

A bird in the hand is worth two in the bush   173

Birds of a feather flock together   172

Buffaloed   89

Bleeding like a stuck pig   46

Blind as a bat   144

Buffaloed   88

Bull dust   82

Bum steer   82

Butterflies in one's stomach   166

Buying a pig in a poke   48

C

A cardinal is a visitor from heaven   176

Cash cow   83

Cat got your tongue?   35

Cat head biscuits   37

A cat may look at a king   31

Cat nap   38

Cats have nine lives   30

The cat's meow   29

The cat's pajamas   29

Catwalk   39

Charley horse   68

Cheeky monkey   131

Chicken-livered   94

Chicken scratches   98

Chick   103

Cock and bull story   78

Cocky   96

Cold enough to kill hogs   44

Cold turkey   114

Copycat   40

Cougar   123

Could talk the horns off a billy goat   93

Crazy as a betsy bug   160

Crazy like a fox   126

Crocodile tears   150

Crook as a dog   17

Crooked as a barrel of snakes   151

Crooked as a dog's hind leg   21

Crow's feet   179

Cry wolf   125

Cunning as a dunny rat   170

Curiosity killed the cat   31

Curses come home to roost   97

Cut off the head of the snake and the body dies   154

D

Dark horse   65

Dead duck   106

Deer-in-the-headlights look   138

Does a cat have a tail?   29

Doesn't have the sense God gave a billy goat   92

Dog and pony show   17

Dog days of summer   19

Dog-eat-dog   10

Dog in the manger   19

A dog is man's best friend   8

Dog leg   21

Dog's body   22

Dog's breakfast   22

Dogs have owners, cats have staffs   31

Dog tired   26

Don't bite the hand that feeds you   11

Don't cast your pearls before swine 48

Don't change horses in the middle of the stream 62

Don't count your chickens before they are hatched 99

Don't keep a dog and bark yourself 13

Don't kick a pullin' mule 77

Don't kill the goose that lays the golden eggs 110

Don't let the fox guard the henhouse 125

Don't look a gift horse in the mouth 70

Drunk as a skunk 143

Dust bunnies 142

Dying duck fit 109

E

Eager beaver 143

Eagle-eyed 175

The eagle flies on Friday 176

Eagles dare to win 175

The early bird catches the worm 174

Eating crow 179

Either fish or cut bait 185

Even a blind pig finds a nut once in a while 51

Every dog has its day 20

Everyone is a genius, but if you judge a fish by its ability to climb a tree, it will spend its whole life thinking it is stupid 190

F

Fat as a pig 43

Feeling one's oats 53

Fine feathered friends 172

A fish always rots from the head down 189

Fish and company always stink after three days 188

A flea in one's ear 162

Flew the coop 101

Forked tongue 152

For the birds 180

Foxhole 126

Fraidy cat / scaredy cat 32

Free as a bird 177

A frog does not drink up the pond in which he lives 149

G

Gag a maggot 163

Gag at a gnat and swallow a camel 137

A game of cat and mouse 34

Get off your high horse 56

Get someone's goat 92

Get the monkey off someone's back 129

Give a man a fish and you'll feed him for a day;
teach a man how to fish
and you'll feed him for a lifetime 184

Go ape over 131

Gobbledygook 113

Going to the dogs 23

Goldfish 42

Gone batty 145

Green around the gills 188

The guilty dog barks first/ loudest 24

Guinea pig 42

Gun shy   16

H

Hair of the dog   22

Happy as a 'possum in a persimmon tree   140

Hatched up   99

Have as many notions as a dog has fleas   18

Have bigger fish to fry   188

He has enough money to burn a wet mule   77

His (or her) bark is worse than his (or her) bite   11

Hog heaven   45

Hogwash   47

Hold your horses   64

Holy cow   84

Hoofing it   63

Hook, line and sinker   185

Horse feathers   68

Horse of a different color   69

Horse sense   67

Horsing around   54

How now brown cow?   84

I

If a rooster crows after sundown,
he will get up with a wet head   100

If it had been a snake it would have bitten you   153

If it walks like a duck, swims like a duck,
and quacks like a duck then it probably is a duck   105

If March comes in like a lion, it goes out like a lamb
If it comes in like a lamb, it goes out like a lion   122

If wishes were fishes, we'd all have a fry   189

If wishes were horses, beggars would ride   60

If you can't bite, never show your teeth   18

If you can't run with the big dogs,
you'd better get off the porch   17

If you lie down with dogs you get up with fleas   18

If you pay peanuts you get monkeys   130

I'll be a monkey's uncle!   130

I've got to see a man about a horse   71

I'm so hungry I could eat a horse   72

In the doghouse 24

It's a dog's life 25

It's hard to soar with the eagles
when you are surrounded by turkeys 113

J

Jailbird 182

Jiminy Cricket! 164

Jive turkey 113

Just chicken feed 98

Just us chickens 103

K

Kangaroo court 139

Kick up one's heels 55

Kill one mosquito and a thousand others
will come to his funeral 160

Kill two birds with one stone 180

King of the jungle 120

Knee-high to a grasshopper 163

L

Lame duck 105

Land on one's feet 36

The law of the jungle 123

Lay an egg 97

The leader of the pack 124

A leopard cannot change its spots 122

Let sleeping dogs lie 9

Let the cat out of the bag 37

Lick one's wounds 14

Like a bat out of hell 145

Like a bull in a china shop 78

Like a chicken with its head cut off 100

Like a dog with a bone 11

Like a duck to water 107

Like a fish out of water 187

Like a lamb to the slaughter 89

Like a lobster pot 192

Like a red rag to a bull 81

Like shooting fish in a barrel   187

Like ugly on an ape   132

Like water off a duck's back   107

Lion hearted   120

Lion's share   121

A little bird told me   176

Living high on/off the hog   45

Loaded for bear   135

Loan shark   190

Lone wolf   124

Looks like the cat that ate the canary 36

Look what the cat dragged in   35

Love birds   177

Lower than a snake's belly   153

M

Mad as a cut snake   155

Madder than a wet hen   96

Make a mountain out of a molehill   146

Male chauvinist pig 47

Mama bear about 135

Milk something or someone 84

Monkey around 127

Monkey business 127

Monkey suit 130

Monkey see, monkey do 128

More fun than a barrel of monkeys 128

Move like the dead lice are falling off of you 163

Mutton dressed as lamb 91

N

Nest egg 98

Never try to teach a pig to sing;
it irritates the pig and wastes your time 50

Never wrestle with a pig.
You both get dirty,
but the pig likes it 50

Nipping at someone's heels 14

No horse in this race 64

No spring chicken 102

O

Oh! What a tangled web we weave
when first we practice to deceive   165

Old goat   92

The old grey mare ain't what she used to be   66

Old warhorse   66

On a short leash   25

One-horse town   71

Open up a can of worms   166

Ought to be horsewhipped   72

P

Pecking order   95

Pick of the litter   40

Pigeon hole   116

Pig-headed   46

Pig-out   44

Play chicken   96

Play 'possum   140

Pony up   75

Poor as Job's turkey 114

Proud as a peacock 115

Pulling a rabbit out of a hat 141

Puppy love 8

Purr like a kitten 33

Pussyfooting around 34

Put out to pasture 86

Putting on the dog 20

Q

Quack 109

Quiet as a mouse 169

Quit horsing around 54

R

Rabbit hole 141

Raining cats and dogs 28

Red herring 191

Riding a hobby horse 58

Riding high   56

Riding off into the sunset   57

Road kill   146

Rode hard and put up wet   57

Root hog or die   49

Rule the roost   96

Run like a scalded dog / cat   13

S

Sacrificial lamb   90

Saddle with   60

Set the cat among the pigeons   36

Sick as a dog   17

Sitting duck   108

Skunk someone   142

Slick as an eel   192

Small fish in a big pond   184

Smarter than the average bear   136

Smell a rat   170

A snail's pace   166

Snake in the grass   151

Snake oil   155

Speaks with a forked tongue   152

Stalking horse   72

Stool pigeon   117

The straw that broke the camel's back   137

Strong as an ox   87

T

Tail between one's legs   14

The tail wagging the dog   15

Take by the scruff of the neck   32

Take the bit between one's teeth   59

Take the bull by the horns   80

Take the reins   59

Talk the hind legs off a donkey   76

Talk turkey   114

That dog won't hunt   16

There is nothing in a caterpillar
that tells you it's going to be a butterfly   165

Throw someone to the lions   121

Tom-catting around   35

Trojan horse   73

Turtles all the way down   149

Two shakes of a lamb's tail   90

U

Ugly duckling   109

W

Walk turkey   113

Wasp waist   161

Watchdog   15

Watch someone like a hawk   182

Weighing the pig doesn't make it any fatter   44

What rock did you crawl out from under?   153

What's sauce for the goose is sauce for the gander   111

When pigs fly   52

When the cat's away the mice will play 168

Which came first, the chicken or the egg? 98

A whistling woman and a crowing hen
always come to no good end 100

White elephant 134

Whole hog or none 48

Why buy a cow when you can get the milk for free? 85

Wild goose chase 111

Wild horses couldn't drag me away 74

A wink's as good as a nod to a blind horse 74

Winner, winner, chicken dinner 103

Wise as an owl 174

A wolf in sheep's clothing 91

Wolf whistle 125

Wouldn't hit a lick at a snake 155

Wouldn't say boo to a goose 112

Wouldn't wish that on a dog 25

Y

You can catch more flies with honey than with vinegar 163

You can feed a pig white truffles
but that doesn't make him a connoisseur 51

You can lead a horse to water
but you can't make it drink 63

You can put lipstick on a pig but it is still a pig 50

You can't make a silk purse out of a sow's ear 50

You can't teach an old dog new tricks 26

You need that like a dog needs side pockets 25

Your goose is cooked 110

When Pigs Fly

www.ingramcontent.com/pod-product-compliance
Lightning Source LLC
Chambersburg PA
CBHW031157270326
41931CB00006B/307

* 9 7 8 1 9 4 7 5 1 4 2 4 9 *